364-2
36

GENEALOGY &  COMPUTERS

*.0

CHARLES CLEMENT
editor

Proceedings of the RASD History Section
Genealogy Committee Program
Reference and Adult Services Division
American Library Association, 9 July 1985

AMERICAN LIBRARY ASSOCIATION
CHICAGO & LONDON, 1986

CS
14
.A44
1985

242998

Composed in Courier Proportional
    on Wang Alliance. Display
    type composed by Pearson
    Typographers.

Printed on 50-pound Glatfelter, a
    pH-neutral stock, and bound in
    10-point Carolina cover
    stock by BookCrafters, Inc.

Library of Congress Cataloging-in-Publication Data

American Library Association. Genealogy Committee.
  Program (1985 : Chicago, Ill.)
  Genealogy and computers.

  Program held July 9, 1985, Chicago, Ill.
  1. Genealogy--Data processing--Congresses.
I. Clement, Charles. II. Title.
CS14.A44 1985   929'.1'0285   85-28016
ISBN 0-8389-3328-9

Printed in the United States of America.

Contents

Preface

Having successfully completed bibliographically oriented programs at San Francisco and Philadelphia, the ALA Genealogy Committee decided to try its hand at a new and very popular combination: genealogy and computers.

Raymond S. Wright of the Genealogical Library in Salt Lake City (and chair of the ALA Genealogy Committee) appointed one to head up a program committee for the 1985 ALA Chicago Conference.

The strategy of the program was to treat the audience to a spectrum of subject content ranging from the very specific, practical, and individual on up to the more theoretical and broad. It was also to include the possibility of actual demonstrations on computers set up in the hall, along with the opportunity to meet with speakers in smaller groups following their presentations.

The presentors were:

Elizabeth Matthews
School of Law Library
Southern Illinois University at
    Carbondale
Carbondale, IL   62901

This paper was specific to individuals who may want to use a personal computer to produce a personal or family history. It was also intended to benefit librarians who are or may in the near future be providing personal computer services in their libraries.

John C. Cosgriff
Newman Library
Virginia Polytechnic Institute
Blacksburg, VA   24061

John wishes that there were online data bases for
genealogy comparable to those for other fields of applied
and social sciences. He effectively demonstrated how one
can use existing data bases to discover genealogical data
in support one's genealogical research.

Robert D. Foster
Systems & Forward Planning
Genealogical Department
Church of Jesus Christ of Latter-day Saints
Salt Lake City, UT   84150

Bob described and demonstrated two things: (1)
GEDCOM, a format for representing genealogical information
so it can be shared among computer systems, and (2) PAF, a
software package for use on home computers.

Keith Stirling and Connie Lamb
Harold B. Lee Library
Brigham Young University
Provo, UT   84602

These two librarians have a burning desire for some
institution important to genealogy to lead in establishing
a standard communication format for genealogical records
and documentation of such. They set forth a proposed
standard based on the MARC format.

Carolyn Leopold Michaels
Office of the Provost
College of Charleston
Charleston, SC   29424

Carolyn effectively summarized and reflected upon the
position taken by each presenter and kept the program
flowing smoothly. Her vast experience in genealogy and in
ALA meetings is always helpful and meaningful.

As a program chair, as a librarian, and as a
genealogist, I was honored to be associated with these
people and this program. Some important tips to
librarians were provided, and issues important to the
field of genealogy and genealogical librarianship were
brought out. As a possible follow-up, a forum including
vendors should seek agreement on a standard communications

format for genealogy. It would be well if at the same
forum genealogical librarians were provided an opportunity
for hands-on demonstration of various genealogical
software packages produced by those vendors.

Charles R. Clement, Program Chair
Genealogical Library
35 N. West Temple
Salt Lake City, UT 84150

New Methods for Old Records

Elizabeth W. Matthews

My assignment is to speak to the aspects of institutional application of computers to genealogy, and/or aspects of the personal application of computers to genealogy, including the practical drawbacks, problems and failures. I shall speak primarily to the very pragmatic application of the institutional computer to genealogy, including drawbacks, problems and potential failures. Then I shall tell you a success saga of personal application.

Having been involved with computerized cataloging of library material for some ten years, and more recently microcomputer applications, I am not surprised to be presenting a paper on computer methods. What is surprising is that I am addressing the subject of genealogy. My first position following college and before attending graduate library school was in a state library as a library assistant. That library was known for its genealogical material and may patrons were doing genealogical research. It seemed to me dull pursuit. I named these intense researchers "The Headhunters," and now I have joined the headhunters, and by presenting this paper, I am admitting it publicly.

COMPUTERS AND GENEALOGY

Those of you who are attending this conference lecture are, no doubt, either assisting patrons in their genealogical research by guiding them to information or working on such research as individuals in private projects. It is possible that there are a few professional genealogists present. In either case, you are very much aware of the large scale computer contributions, such as those originating from Salt Lake City, where the computer has made access to local and international records possible by means of the International Genealogical Index, previously the Computer File Index. The Genealogical Department has offered information from other tools, such as the Temple Records Index Bureau and Family Group Records Archive. It has provided safekeeping for the storage of those records, and it has made records available in branch libraries by means of fiche and film. In addition, its vast collection is described by means of the MOC, or microfilmed card catalog, now being replaced by the GLC, or Genealogical Library Catalog, on fiche.

We want to look at the more personalized utilization of computers for genealogical projects, especially microcomputers. For the moment we shall overlook minicomputers which stand somewhere between mainframe and microcomputers. Personal and microcomputers can be utilized to advantage in specialized projects, such as genealogical storage and publishing. Some genealogists have discovered lap computers for use in data gathering, transcribing in the field. Some have learned to transfer the data to desk top computers. Many librarians are in the process of acquiring or have already acquired micro-computers for library utilization. Others have acquired microcomputers for patron use, some of which are the coin-operated variety, enjoyed by the population just as coin operated typewriters had been utilized in libraries in the past. A recent issue of Library Journal describes coin-operated APPLES provided by COMPUMAT at a public library.[1] In at least one law school library coin-operated DECMATES were provided and utilized successfully until numerous microcomputers were provided for student use without charge at work processing stations. It is left to your imagination to figure out which one remained by popular demand until a reasonable fee was instigated.[2] According to the February issue of Library Journal, approximately 44 percent of the public libraries make their microcomputers available to the public; college

---

1. "News in Review," Library Journal 110 (Jan. 1, 1985): 38.
2. "The Impact of Law and Computers on the Law Teacher," Association of American Law Schools Law and Computers Section Newsletter 1 (Fall 1984): 9.

and university libraries provide them in 46 percent of
the cases and 26 percent of the special libraries provide
this convenience. Not all of the micros are used on
location as a few libraries (only 2.5 percent) permit
the machines to be checked out for home use.[3]
     Some librarians are contemplating the purchase of
microcomputers which will be utilized by patrons in
genealogical and other projects. A number of genealogists
already have their own personal computers. Andereck
reported findings of a survey of 1500 subscribers to
Genealogical Computing, with 50% response rate, that 635,
or 84% owned computers.[4] This might have been the
anticipated response, however, since persons primarily
interested in computers and genealogy would be subscribing
to such a journal. Perhaps those of you with personal
computers are already busy inputting your own records.
Occasionally, one sees reference to one of the early
problems in computerized libraries. There were staff
members who cold not resist inputting their own records.
If you are granted the privilege of utilizing the
institutional computer for individual projects after
business hours, that is another matter.
     Microcomputers accessible to the public provide a new
dimension to their research. Librarians have assisted
patrons in using reference tools, in obtaining census
reports and other primary resources from the National
Archives by means of interlibrary loan, and now there is
the opportunity to assist in the organizing, storing, and
disseminating the results of patron research. In the
continuing education aspects of libraries, what better
place is there for microcomputers than in the library,
where there is or can be expert guidance?
     The kind of microcomputer available varies from
library to library, even from model to model within
libraries. Does your library contain APPLES, RAINBOWS,
BLUEBIRDS, DEC, NED, IBM, etc.? What kind of software
does it have? Some libraries are acquiring enormous
amounts of software, some system packages and data files
of importance in subject areas. In at least one library
micro center use increased from some 1300 to more than
3000 in a seven-month period, and software loan
transactions more than doubled in six months. That
library's software collection accounts for 10% of the
library loan activity.[5] With so many patrons using a

     3.   John Berry, "Library Use of Micro-computers:
Massive & Growing," Library Journal 110 (Feb. 1, 1985): 48.
     4.   Paul Andereck, Genealogical Computing: The
Beginning (Fairfax, Va.: Data Transfer, 1984) pp. 4-21.
     5.   Howard Curtis, "The Mann Library Microcomputer
Center," Small Computers in Libraries, 4 (Dec. 1984): 9.

micro center or borrowing software from it for use on
their own computers, there must be some advantages to
computer use. What are those advantages?

Advantages

The advantages are great. One can be a poor typist
and provide fine copy by utilizing a microcomputer with
random access, which permits input, additions, and
changes. One can proofread on screen or paper printout
and correct easily, without the usual investment in cases
of correction fluid. One can move blocks of text, repeat,
center phrases, provide superscript and subscript, add
footnotes, change format by altering margins or spacing,
highlight phrases with bold type or underlining. And all
of those words can be tested against an automatic
speller. Some machines will alphabetize, sort, do global
searches and changes, and add phrase libraries. Other
features include automatic paging, running titles,
indexing, label making, and maintaining lists. The
material which has been stored can be updated easily
before a new edition.

With improvement of disk technology, in which a
magnetic head presses over the lateral disk surface,
storage capacity is increasing. It can provide the
records management which genealogists need. A prototype
has the capability of storing up to five million
characters, and is expected on the market in 1985;
perpendicular storage is scheduled for the future
according to the Library Systems Newsletter. The
recording surface would be thicker than that in
traditional format, supporting vertical recording of data,
thereby providing denser storage.[6] Presently, floppy
disks have limited storage capacity, which is normally
between one hundred thousand and one million characters or
bytes. The size of disks varies from three to eight
inches, with those of five-and-a-quarter size being the
most popular, making possible storage of some 250 pages of
text, or approximately 500,000 characters. (An APPLE II
single disk holds 143,000 characters, or 95 pages of text
at 25 lines per page and 60 characters per line; IBM PC
holds 360,000 characters, or 240 pages.)[7] Andereck
suggests that the eight-inch disk is most desirable for
family files since it can accommodate more records.[8] As
one might expect, it is more expensive and requires a disk

---

6. Library Systems Newsletter, (Dec. 4, 1984): 91
7. David H. Carlson "The Perils of Personals,"
Library Journal 110 (Feb. 1, 1985): 52.
8. Andereck, pp. 4-57.

drive to accommodate it. A disk drive can be as expensive as the computer.

Subject specific software, which was lacking, has become available fairly recently. It can provide the records management necessary in genealogy and it can produce charts as needed. Among the most popular genealogical software can be found: ROOTS/M, FAMILY ROOTS, GENSYSTEMS, PEDIGREE/PRT, GENEAL, COMPILROOTS, and GENIE.[9] A recent announcement regarding FAMILY ROOTS emphasizes the fact that it is a comprehensive integrated package for genealogists, from beginners to advanced. Testimonials tracked down and reported by Library Journal indicated that persons utilizing the software in several public libraries have no complaints or problems to report.[10] Leith, in Creative Computing, speaks favorably concerning the program as well and mentions its descent from LINEAGES. He describes it as a group of interlinked programs on the two disks, written in modifiable Basic. Illustrations of the charts are included.[11]

On an APPLE II one can use THE GENEALOGISTS RIGHT HAND software to interrelate names of persons on one disk to another disk. Some software, such as the ACORN products, can produce a three-generation ancestor chart and a pedigree chart with a single line of descent. It can provide search by full or partial names, by country, state, county, or year. It can print the charts as well, and ANCESTRY I/III provides standard forms. Although it would be a great convenience to have this specific software for compiling and maintaining individual data sheets, family group sheets, lineage charts, and ancestor tables, standard software for a personal computer can be utilized for text, data storage, and retrieval capabilities. The general word processing, text formatting, and data base management programs would be standard for inputting history notes, writing correspondence, maintaining lists, and indexing. Using a little ingenuity one could improvise with charts or order those from another source to be used with the created text.

The forms for questionnaires used for data gathering in the present generation population can be constructed by means of microcomputer. After layout is planned for absolute clarity of the instrument, attention can focus on margins, space, lines, headings, inserts, and directions.

9.   Ibid., pp. 4-58.
10.   "Tracing Family Roots With Software Package," Library Journal 110 (Feb. 1, 1984): 24.
11.   J. Douglas Leith, "Put a Computer on Your Family Tree," Creative Computing 10 (May 1984): 102-8.

If properly constructed, with regard for semantics, such a questionnaire can elicit the information sought and encourage a high response rate.[12]

Disadvantages
    Having a number of the advantages, computers must have a few disadvantages. Yes, the system is not foolproof, as yet. What can happen, some of which probably will happen? Material can be lost. After you have input, corrected, edited, added footnotes and bibliography, it can happen. My colleague lost an entire article, bibliography included.

If a tape or disk, floppy disk, or diskette, by whatever name, is exposed to a magnet, it is gone. Just placing your disk near a device containing magnetism can automatically erase everything you have so patiently, or impatiently, input, and such devices very seldom have a label, reading "Magnet." Your text can be wiped out in a moment. Not only the price of your disk is involved, but more than simply money has been lost when you consider the time element.

The disk must not be exposed to extreme heat or cold. This sounds easy, but is your library always at even temperature? Has the power ever gone off in January in a cold climate, or the air conditioning in the Deep South in mid-summer? These things can affect your disk if it is stored in the building. If you choose residential storage or have patrons store their own disks, these changes in temperature are likely to have impact on the disk storage. For those who choose to carry the disk from home to library, temperature changes while the disk is in transit must be observed. Although permanently encased in rigid plastic, it must be kept in its paper envelope, as well. This offers little protection and it is better placed in addition into a specially manufactured disk container. The quality of the disk is important too, taking into account discolorations, the result of inadequate polishing which can result in disk drive wear, the strength of the electrical signal transferred to the disk, and the inclusion of a tight hub around the center hole of the disk compensating for mechanical disk drive misalignment.

As most of you are aware, information stored on the disk can be damaged if the disk itself is touched on the exposed part, and it is most often exposed in two areas. Labeling the disk carries certain dangers, as well. Since

---

    12.   Elizabeth   W.   Matthews.   Questionnaire Construction for Maximum Survey Response, ERIC Doc. ED 170006, 1979.

librarians are prone to label items, and rightly so, it must be done with care. No pencil, pen, or stylus should be used to record the name or code of the documents or even to note your ownership of the disk. A felt point pen can be utilized safely to label the disk, since there would not be a sharp edge which could cut through, damaging the fragile magnetic surface underneath.

Smoke is especially damaging to the disk, and while the disk is being utilized in the microcomputer, smoking should not be permitted in the room. (I have probably lost half of the audience with this statement.) It has been shown, however, that the smoke particles cover the fragile lateral surface and damage it.

There are many steps to remember before you even get to the command keys. Once you have learned to turn on the microcomputer and have inserted the disk, you must remember at the end of the session to remove the disk before powering down. (There are exceptions to this, in the IBM 300, for instance.) Then, too, you must remember which disk drive to use in the case of dual disk drive, or which of four if you are utilizing a more powerful machine courtesy of your institution. The system disk is placed in the first position and your data disk in the second or other disk drive. After you have input your data, it is of utmost importance to end your session properly. It is possible to lose everything you have input during a particular session, be it minutes or hours, if you do not use the proper phrase or term "file" the document. You will remember this after losing a lengthy bibliography! Virtually every make and model differs in the way a record must be filed for storage and retrieval. And the simple human error of inadvertently erasing the input by using the incorrect command key can happen, in spite of prompts which are often included. So much for the disk dissertation.

Do not forget to make a backup copy of any material which you have input. (This was meaningless to me until I began inputting this paper. After a disk crashed containing ten pages for which I had no backup, this statement has special meaning.) A backup copy is accomplished by merely inputting a blank disk into the disk drive and using the "copy" command, thereby copying from your data disk to another or blank disk. (I know of a case in which the original disk was considered backup, the paper printout sent off to a publishing house. The system disk was bad; therefore when the data disk was inserted and utilized, it was ruined. The author had but one recourse--to ask the publisher to send a copy of the manuscript.) To prevent such an occurrence due to defective disk drives, there is a new early warning system package available for several micro models which evaluates the disk drive for speed, noise tolerance, write-read, track alignment, positioner backlash, disk clamping, and erase crosstalk.[13]

Some software is not usable for long documents. BENCHMARK, for example, has the warning in its instruction manual that no document longer than ten pages should be input. That is not enough space to contain my genealogy! Is it enough for you? If such information is disregarded, that occupied storage space beyond the ten pages and indeed the entire document could be lost. What does lost mean? Not recovered! No longer there! Input again!

Another hazard is in losing information which is on the disk if the power goes off or fluctuates while your disk is being used. It does the system disk no good to have a power outage. Power surges interfere with operation of the micro and recording of data. There are surge suppressors which can be attached to eliminate such surges. If the power goes off, there are devices to save you from losing "data in the dark." The advertisements mention uninterruptible power supplies. This would keep you from losing a long file when a sudden power outage occurs. One suggestion offered in BYTE for temporary retention is by way of battery. It seems unlikely that many individuals would connect such batteries. It is a short term solution anyhow, providing only temporary storage, and useful only if power is off during a brief interim. The unprotected hardware may already have experienced a crash.[14] Another suggestion is to use sources of power independent of the local public utility which switches over to a supply only when your power fails. Our institution does not have one, and it is doubtful that many individuals would have such an auxiliary device. One method of safeguard is by using a system whereby updating of records is done by using an allocated block of disk space, rather than by overwriting, although this method requires more disk space.[15]

Although your information may have survived the periods of input and be safely sorted, a few scholars are concerned about what will eventually happen to present-day floppy disks. The library archivist at Duke University, for instance, is not at all certain that disks will be

13.   Southern Illinois University Computing Affairs Newsletter (Jan. 1985): 9.

14.   William Rynone, "Uninterruptible Power Supplies," BYTE 10 (Jan. 1985): 183-84.

15.   Charles Daney and Tom Forth, "A Tale of Two Operation Systems, BYTE IBM Issue Guide to the IBM Personal Computer (Fall 1984): 43.

readable by hardware of the future, due to incompatibility
of new machines. He is concerned as well that the
information stored thereon will require constant update,
encoding into different format that might be compatible
with new machines. He points to the fact that historians
and archivists have seldom been consulted regarding
long-time storage by tape or disks.[16]
Some publishers are willing to receive a disk and
publish directly from that. If the publisher's hardware
differs, so that our disk does not conform, a transfer can
be arranged (for instance for NEC disk to IBM disk in a
transaction which takes only a few minutes). As the disk
travels, is it safe? Is it protected from magnetic
fields? There is the case of the author, too worried to
send magnetic tapes through the mail, who took it by air.
After passing through the checkpoint, a magnetic device
removed all that was stored and he arrived with a blank!
He could have protected his information with a lead-lined
container, or by circumventing the magnetic checkpoint.
Furthermore, many word processing programs have the means
for writing an unformatted ASCII file onto the author's
diskette for later transmission from the author's computer
to a communications port on the publisher's text editing
system.[17]
Having noted all of these elements involved, are you
willing to provide microcomputers without software for
your patrons? If you decide to do it, will they bring the
required supplies, or will you furnish them, sell them,
charge them? How will you store their disks, the system
disks? Do you have a few in a box or do you have numerous
pieces which should be cataloged according to the new AACR
2 machine-readable format?

HARDWARE

Printers
After you have input and properly stored information
on a disk, you are ready for the printout. One quickly
learns the command "print." The selection process
involves choice of dot matrix or letter quality impact
printer, usually with a daisy wheel. One must learn how

16. "An Archivist Worries About Floppy Disks,"
Chronicle of Higher Education (20 Feb. 1985): 16.
17. "How to Lose Money Electronically," Library
Journal 109 (Nov. 15 1984): 2125-28; John P. Rash, "How to
Lose Money With Ignorance," Library Journal 110 (Feb. 1,
1985): 6. See also: Sidney B. Geller. Care and Handling
of Computer Magnetic Storage Media (Washington: National
Bureau of Standards, 1983).

to replace the daisy wheel and have spares on hand. And are you going to use single sheets or continuous feed? If you are providing printers for patrons, as surely as one has used single sheets, another will require continuous feed, thereby requiring some adjustment of equipment, which may not be conveniently arranged. It is possible for the printer to be connected to more than one machine, thereby, requiring the changing of a switch by means of a "t-switch" or similar device.

These are complicated machines as well, so that one can go into background with printer operating for one person while work continues on that or an adjacent machine for input. Be forewarned that a good ribbon is a must in the final printout, although a practice ribbon can be used a number of times in the editing process. After all is set and the printer is in motion, sheets feeding through in clear bold print, all you have to do is to sit back and wait. While some persons leave for other duties in the interim, it is wise to check the printout.

You or your patron will soon have camera-ready copy. Then you have it made, provided you can find a commercial printer or even a publisher for your manuscript. With this whole genre of material self-publishing is the most utilized method of dissemination. Few publishing houses are interested in your genealogy, although you recognize its importance and true worth.

Microcomputer Terminals

If you decide to provide hardware for use, it would be wise to peruse Crawford's checklist of visual display terminals, based on the CRT terminal checklist.[18] While software has increased in price, the hardware, with new features and greater memory, has become less expensive. The outlined steps to selection could be applied to computer terminals or to personal computer selection. In the first step, one should evaluate individual needs and develop criteria, establishing minimum acceptability. Crawford suggests planning for a short term rather than too long a term, while Andereck encourages open-ended choices so that later a modem or hard disk could be added for additional storage space. Crawford then suggests a practical worksheet, with weighting and comparisons between models. He insists upon a budget range and knowing the number of devices required. Next, he suggest surveying the market by consulting trade journals, in particular, microcomputer magazines. In addition to

18.   Walt Crawford, "VDT Checklist : Another Look at Terminals, Information Technology and libraries 3 (Dec. 1984):   343-53; Crawford, "CRT Terminal Checklist," Journal of Library Automation 13 (March 1980): 36-44.

checking our computer stores, observing displays at
conferences would be informative. Then Crawford suggests
observation and use, followed by talking to the actual
users themselves. In our subject of interest, this would
include genealogists who have computer and computer
programs, preferably those with some experience. For
those interested in a computer for genealogical purposes,
the journal Genealogical Computing carries practical
information, and it is possible that the new bimonthly
MicroRoots will be useful in this regard. In a guide to
microcomputer literature, Pratt has noted that literature
for a specific profession is virtually impossible to track
down and suggests contacting the professional society in
the area of interest for such information.[19]

Other features of the terminal which should be checked
out include screen width (from 32 to 80 characters), the
number of lines (24 being a popular choice), availability
of letters with upper and lower case character legibility,
screen color, positive or negative polarity, glare, and
flicker, detachability, angle of keyboards, and special
keys.

As you set up work stations, you will be involved in
the whole area of "ergonomics," defined as comfort in
height, seating, viewing distances, work surfaces,
lighting, glare and other details.[20] Your patron will
probably be so engrossed in inputting his genealogical
material that he will be oblivious to all of this, so
intense is his concentration. I can tell you this with
the voice of experience, and with that I shall describe
briefly the successful publishing of a genealogy by
computer methods.

SUCCESS SAGA

Yes, my scraps of paper were numerous and contained
the usual hieroglyphics. There were documented snatches,
from various times, various places, whole sheets and
tablets fortunately footnoted. These accumulated. Being
a librarian, I tend to take a busman's holiday, prowling
libraries head hunting and searching for answers to
burning research questions. When it was no longer
possible to locate individual scraps among the mounds of

---

19.   Allan D. Pratt, A Selective Guide to the
Microcomputer Literature (Tucson: Graham Conley Press,
1983), p. 4.
20.   Louis Tijerina, Video Display Terminal
Workstation Ergonomics ([Dublin, Ohio] OCLC Online
Computer Library Center, 1984).

paper I had collected, I prepared eight, no, I should say sixteen folders, and began to toss the scraps into the folders depending on which surname was the focus of entry. Does this remind you of filing? I can assure you they were not in alphabetical order. Then followed a measure of color coding which I found helpful. A rough typing followed, bringing like material together (the classifier). Ordinarily, the piece would have been typed again. Instead I utilized the word processor, an early digital model, after obtaining the proper permission, of course, for this after-hours project.

It was necessary to purchase the diskette for $12, the ribbon for $6, and more ribbons for $6; the paper added up too. Although this word processor had been used for a book which I had published on utilization of the card catalog in law libraries, a student had done the input for that. However, I had input an article, and that only after listening to a lecture setting forth instructions for operation. I tried out those instructions as noted later. My directions were basic. They began, "Get my disk!" So you can see that I was no expert. It was not difficult to learn standard input/output procedures and control key commands. I inserted the new disk, initialized it before beginning any input, named the document, set up margins, indicated spacing, and began. Patience was the difficult requirement, and there were times when I wished for an optical scanner which would more or less "vacuum" up the material without actual input.

I remembered to start the power before inserting the disks, to boot it, to utilize the command keys. Although the basic keyboard was not at all different from the typewriter, the importance of "insert" and "delete" could not be overlooked. Having used OCLC for a number of years, I found some of these commands logical. There were special commands for the use of superscript, footnote numbers, underlining, and for centering, and I learned to "cut and paste" electronically, which moved blocks of print. Finally, I "finished" or "filed" the document after each session. If I had not done that, the entire text which I had input during that session would have been erased.

I was bold enough to press the "print" key, only after inserting the paper and putting on the correct print style daisy wheel and the practice ribbon. All of these steps were necessary almost every time the word processor was used. And it was used many times. After completing the work period each time, I removed the data disk and the system disk and stored them in their envelopes and in their cases. Fortunately, the system disk was housed close by. I kept my data disk in my briefcase, in spite of the dire warnings of its being fragile and subject to temperature changes. It very nearly became a permanent fixture. Wherever it went, I went; and wherever I went, it went. It occupied the passenger seat of my car, always the briefcase in upright position. No passenger dared to usurp the seat occupied by The Disk, carrying ancestral characters. On the coldest day, my scarf was around the briefcase and I was the one reduced to freezing.

Chapter by chapter, all eight were finally input. And it was a long document. That meant that searching was particularly time consuming. Yes, the machine would search my disk for a term, but it was very slow, and stopped searching after about fifty pages. That meant that I had to wait listening to the slow click, click, as each page was read by the magnetic head. It took about one half hour to locate anything as far as page 110. It would have been better if I had input several short documents.

Yes, I experienced an electrical power outage. A storm was on the horizon, although it was not obvious to one in an inside office. During that particular session, I lost everything I had input during those hours, but fortunately, not everything which I had input up to that time. Actually, very often, I did a printout so that I had at least that much information. In the early and editing stages, I input a great deal of information which was not written down anywhere, as my style is to think at the keyboard.

The microcomputer, or word processor, used a lot of paper. I could not merely erase a letter, but I had to go into the data base and correct a word or a single letter and print the entire page as necessary.

I found the final pagination difficult, working manually on page breaks, so that there would not be a single word or phrase left at the top of any one page. Finally, I added the contents with pagings, and input the index. While some microcomputers will index, the word processing portion of this would not. Therefore, after listing names manually and having scrutinized each page, I alphabetized those manually and input them. There are better ways. As you have gathered by now, no genealogy specific software was available, and I was using a general text program. Finally, the last word was input and the last mistake wiped out. The camera ready copy was ready. At this point, I had time to reflect on the contrast of the modern computer output with several leaves of early manuscript materials, replicas of originals included as illustrations: a muster of 1812; a will dated 1830; and early inventory, deed, and contract.

The only real problem was in the binding of the book.

I had preferred a "book" size and not 8 x 11; therefore, I reduced the print which had come from the letter quality printer. The numerous copies, after being duplicated, were sent off to the binder with instructions for trimming. The binder was on a computer, and obviously there was neither interface nor face-to-face. You can imagine my surprise as I tore open the boxes of books to see large 8 x 11 binders covering the little 6 x 9 pages. Needless to say, they were returned and it took considerable explanation to get the right size. But the second time around the top margins were cut too close and the shadows at the bottom which should have been removed, were left intact. What has been cut cannot be restored. That slight imperfection I have had to accept. The persons interested in the information contained therein have not complained, and perhaps it is such a fascinating book, they have not even noticed!

CONCLUSION

Do you want to assist your patrons with such a project? It is worthwhile, and this whole genre of material depends on this type of publishing. Will you select the micro and the software, provide the ribbon, pick a daisy wheel, provide paper, watch for power surges, and see to the printing? And what will you do about closing time, when a patron's long document is being printed page after page, grinding from the machine. Would you have enough nerve to close? On that note I too shall close.

MARGEDOS: A MARC-like Format for Genealogy

Keith H. Stirling and
Connie Lamb

Information handling is a prime area in which computer technology is used for storing and retrieving recorded information, and genealogy has not been overlooked as an application. Genealogical data--names, dates, vital data, relationships,and sources--can readily be stored, manipulated, and retrieved. In a matter of seconds information is entered, changed, or called up via the computer that would take hours to do manually. As genealogists gather pieces of data and expand the genealogical tree, it becomes challenging to organize the materials and allow for ready access. It is no surprise, then, that genealogy would be a logical application for computers.

However, the wide variety of genealogical data sources and finding aids matched with the variability in experience of those who use these sources suggests the existence of a number of bibliographic problems--problems especially familiar to the librarian. Anytime one attempts to link together the creators of information with the consumers of information one discovers how imperfect language representations are. The construction of indexes, classification schemes, syndetic and other finding aids is an attempt to bridge the communication gap between the creator and consumer, but most persons do not know how to use them.

With respect to genealogical data, the need exists for a universal communication format--one which permits genealogical data to be communicated among both people and machines. This paper presents a concept, familiar to librarians, for intellectual access to and control of genealogical data.

THE NATURE OF GENEALOGICAL RECORDS

Genealogical records have some unique characteristics that make them different from other data. For instance, their data structures must provide for the existence of family relationships by linking together an individual record. These linkages must extend both forward and backward in time--tying together parents with children--as well as providing horizontal linkages with spouses. There are three types of genealogical records: individual, family group sheets, and pedigree charts. Although the basic unit record focuses on the individual, it also contains the necessary information to achieve both of the more complex record types.

One requisite for organizing genealogical data is the need to provide a tracking system which allows one to establish the accuracy of individual data elements. The search for written records is the crux of the genealogist's work, but these sources may contain discrepancies. For example, during a person's lifetime many records are created which state his or her birthdate because it is an essential item for identification. However, variations in that information may occur due to imperfect memory, recording, or transcription. The genealogist who is trying to document an individual's vital information is faced with the same problems as the historian. Does the source in hand represent a faithful, primary recording of the event or is it a secondary record? The most correct recording would seem to be the one closest in time to the event, but that one may not always be available. As new evidences come to light how may these be compared with existing documentation so that the most accurate, composite record of the individual may be constructed?

In addition, the geometrics of genealogy are amazing. In just a few generations, theoretically, hundreds of people could be searching for the same individual. Several persons, for example, who may be working on the same line, may have access to different sources which could result in conflicting individual records. Their efforts may result in variations of spellings, dates, places, etc. Because of these problems, it is important that documentation be supplied with the records in order that these inconsistencies may be evaluated.

Genealogical records differ among various cultures,

and individuals in those cultures may record information
in a variety of ways. This lack of standardization can be
a problem as records are brought together from many places
into one large file. If computers must accept the
different formats used to communicate this information, it
is mandatory that some degree of standardization be
obtained. The questions then become, "How important is
the quality of the record?", "Do we want accuracy and/or
the capability to discriminate between sources of data
when discrepancies exist?", and if so, "What should be the
standard communication format?"

MACHINE-READABLE DOCUMENTATION

A viable solution for providing genealogical data
standards similar to those required by librarians for
bibliographic control may be achieved, but it probably
will come at a price similar to what they have paid. What
is the price for genealogical record control? Those who
are familiar with this path sense that a long-term
commitment is required.
Devising a solution doesn't make much sense unless it
provides flexibility in documentation--thus accommodating
the wide range in quality of sources encountered by a
researcher, yet at the same time providing one the
capability to construct a better quality record based upon
accumulated evidences. A flexible solution should permit
full documentation for each field within an individual
record while permitting inter unit-record conflicts to
exist when more than one record on an individual is
present. Then when variability and conflict among the
records exists--together with the documentation for these
data--an analysis and judgment can be made as to what data
is most accurate. This, however, means that increased
storage space is needed. It also means that additional
personal time is required to resolve the conflicts. The
bright side, however, is that, manually, the task would be
burdensome if not impossible for an individual
researcher. How do librarians maintain intellectual
access to and control over their bibliographic data? What
can we learn from their experience?
The computer allows one to sift through large
quantities of data in machine-readable format to identify
deficiencies and inconsistencies. In the library field,
we have a well-known mechanism for doing this with
bibliographies-namely, MARC, the Machine-Readable
Cataloging format developed by the Library of Congress.
The concept the authors are using to maintain genealogical
control is based upon the MARC format. This system was

chosen because of its familiarity and, more importantly, because of its capability to maintain intellectual control over the data. It is adaptable to genealogy and the concept is easy to understand. Essentially, the MARC format organizes the individual data elements of a record and indexes these to permit ready access through automated retrieval.

The original genealogical version of a MARC-like format which provides documentation of sources is named MARGEDOS, an acronym for Machine-Readable Genealogy with Documentation of Sources.[1] The data elements of MARGEDOS coincide with those of the family group record. In addition, data elements are defined for the inclusion of complete documentation. Not only are the various elements of data within a record distinctly recorded and indexed but so also are the sources from which the data was derived such that both can be easily retrieved with the aid of the computer.

Since the original definition of MARGEDOS, experience has suggested that machine readable-genealogical documentation is more easily represented if the records are based upon the individual rather than the family unit. Linkages can easily be established between individual records to represent more complex relationships. Moreover, we have switched from numeric codes to mnemonic ones so that the meaning of individual data fields will be readily apparent to the observer. Our revised format is called MARGEDOS II, but will be referred to as MARGEDOS in what follows. MARGEDOS makes possible the ability to detect inconsistencies within genealogical records and the ability to create more accurate records by merging into one record those field supported by primary evidence but which may be scattered throughout numerous duplicate records.

MARGEDOS DEFINED

Like LC's MARC record, the MARGEDOS format consists of three sections: Leader, Record Directory, and Variable Field. The fixed length leader communicates information about the specific record which follows. Information such as the length of the genealogical record in MARGEDOS form, where the variable field portion of the record begins, and the length of the subfield codes if contained therein. Additional space is also provided for items which may be defined at some future date.

---

1. Connie Lamb and Keith H. Stirling, "A Communication Format for Automated Documentation in Genealogy," Genealogical Journal (Mar. 1979): 34-42.

The second segment, the record directory, is a series of coded units corresponding to fields within the genealogical record. Each coded unit contains a mnemonic tag, which identifies the meaning of its respective field length and the other identifying the starting position of the field within the variable field portion of the record. A list of data field codes, their tags, and their subfield codes is given in Table 1. The directory permits a computer to build multiple indexes to each genealogical record and search an entire data base of records for specific indexed attributes corresponding to information need.

The variable fields that make up the third section include the data from the genealogical records. Each of the data fields located on the individual record is assigned to one of the fields within this section of the MARGEDOS record. Again, the data fields and the documentation for the data files are indexed by their corresponding codes in the record directory. If necessary, each data field is further subdivided by a series of subfield codes which identify individual field elements also needing to be indexed. So each data element is machine searchable via a two-level index, its corresponding record directory and then individual subfield codes. Figure 1 is an example of a MARGEDOS record. Note that because of the subfield code definitions, the category codes for MARGEDOS are fewer in number than the field codes used in DIALTWIG, and, consequently, may not have the same meaning in the two systems.

The fields for each component of the record are of variable length rather than fixed length. This means that the information stored in each field contains as many characters as are necessary to record the known data. No space is lost due to missing or incomplete data. Moreover, MARGEDOS does permit additional data to be added at a later date simply by making appropriate adjustments in the variable field and the record directory, then rewriting the record.

In summary, the MARGEDOS record is based on the individual with one record for each person containing all of their genealogical data. Each record (name) is given in a unique accession number. To establish relationships between individual's records the accession numbers corresponding to the individual's parents and spouse and children are included in his or her record. This means that a person using the system can move in either direction through the file beginning with an individual record. The movement can be up to parents, down to children, or across to spouses. Multiple entries are permitted on appropriate fields to accommodate divorces, additional marriages, adoptions, etc.[2]

---

2. Note that it is imperative that the integrity of the accession numbers be maintained as each must uniquely

Leader				Record Directory						
00858		00182	2	NA	0038	00000	GD	0002	00038	BI	0035

| 00040 | ZI | 0035 | 00075 | DE | 0035 | 00110 | MA | 0075 | 00145 | FA | 0036 |

| 00220 | MO | 0035 | 00256 | CH | 0124 | 00291 | SB | 0049 | 00415 | SZ | 0049 |

| 00415 | SD | 0052 | 00464 | SM | 0061 | 00516 | SP | 0046 | 00577 | SC | 0053 |

Variable Fields

00623^ $aHarrison, Josephine Asenath$b85AAAA^ F^

$a12 Dec$b1890$cOgden$dWeber$eUtah^ $a17 Sep$b1899$cOgden

$dWeber$eUtah^ $a11 Mar$b1921$cOgden$dWeber$eUtah^

$a09 Sep$b1908$cSalt Lake City$dSalt Lake$eUtah$fWhite,

David John$g85AAAB^ $aHarrison, Joseph Johnston$b85AAAC^

$aTillotson, Elizabeth Ann$b85AAAD^ $1White, Josephine

Arlean $a85AAAE$2White, Elva Elizabeth$b85AAAF$3White,

Elmer David$c85AAAG$4White, LeRoy Charles$d85AAAH^

$aLDS MEM REC$bOgden 4th Ward$c#26230$d1877-1918^

$aOBIT NOTICE$bOgden Standard Examiner$d13 Mar 1921^

$aMARR CERTIFICATE$bSalt Lake City, Utah$c#4198$d09 Sep 1908^

$aMARR APPLICATION$bWeber County$d08 Sep 1908^

$aOLDS MEM REC$bOOgden 4th Ward$cO#26230$dO1877-1918^

Fig. 1. Full genealogical record in MARGEDOS format

identify one and only one individual. In MARGEDOS the
accession number begins with the year the record is
entered into the file as given by two digits (e.g. 85).
That number is followed by four alpha characters which
allows for about one-half million records to be entered
each year. The numbering system goes 85AAAA, 85AAAB,
85AAAC, ... 85ZZZZ. If that number of records proved to
be too small or too large, adjustments could be made in
the system.

Table 1. Definition of MARGEDOS Field and Subfield Codes

Data Field Name	Code	Subfield Codes			
Name	NA	$a	Name	$b	Accession No.
Gender	GD	none			
Birth Information	BI	$a	Day, Month	$b	Year
		$c	City/Town	$d	County
		$e	State/Province		
Christening Info.	YI	$a	Day, Month	$b	Year
		$c	City/Town	$d	County
		$e	State/Province		
Baptismal Info.	ZI	$a	Day, Month	$b	Year
		$c	City/Town	$d	County
		$e	State/Province		
Death Information	DE	$a	Day, Month	$b	Year
		$c	City/Town	$d	County
		$e	State/Province		
Interment (burial)	IN	$a	Day, Month	$b	Year
		$c	City/Town	$d	County
		$e	State/Province		
Marriage Info.		$a	Day, Month	$b	Year
		$c	City/Town	$d	County
		$e	State/Province		
		$f	Spouse Name	$g	Accession No.
Father	FA	$a	Name	$b	Accession No.
Mother	MO	$a	Name	$b	Accession No.
Children	CH	$1	Name 1st chld	$a	Accession No.
		$2	Name 2nd chld	$b	Accession No.
		$3	Name 3rd chld	$c	Accession No.
			etc.		
Source, Birth	SB	$a	Record type	$b	Place/Location
		$c	ID #	$d	Date
Source, Christening	SY	$a	Record type	$b	Place/Location
		$c	ID #	$d	Date
Source Baptism	SZ	$a	Record type	$b	Place/Location
		$c	ID #	$b	Date
Source Death	SD	$a	Record type	$b	Place/Location
		$c	ID #	$d	Date
Source, Interment	SI	$a	Record type	$b	Place/Location
		$c	ID #	$d	Date
Source, Marriage	SM	$a	Record type	$b	Place/Location
		$c	ID #	$d	Date
Source, Parents	SP	$a	Record type	$b	Place/Location
			ID #	$d	Date
Source, Children	SC	$an	Record type	$bn	Place/Location
		$cn	ID #	$dn	Date
		where "n" corresponds to the child's number. If n = 0, then use same source for all children.			

DIALTWIG DEFINED

DIALTWIG is an information retrieval system which accepts
the MARGEDOS records as input, creates full text access by
field to these records, and permits this information to be
displayed in a variety of different formats. It permits one
to search genealogical records using boolean logic similar to
the well-known online bibliographic search services. A
two-letter mnemonic code is used to tag each field and can be
used to limit searches to particular data fields. Different
display formats are provided so that various portions of the
record can be called up on the screen or printer. For
example, a search could be done combining a name and a
birthdate or a name and a place. If there are several hits,
one display format, which selects the birth place, birth
date, names of parents and spouse could be displayed--thus
helping to establish the identity of each. Another display
format is used to select and display the source documentation
for the different data fields. The names of parents,
children, and spouse for each record (if they are known) are
linked through accession numbers so that DIALTWIG may display
these related records. More information concerning this
general purpose micro-based retrieval system may be obtained
from the School of Library and Information Science, Brigham
Young University, Provo, UT 84602.

A SCENARIO

Having machine-readable access to the fields of the
genealogical records one may resolve conflicts that appear in
them. In this case we used DIALTWIG. Consider, for example,
the following situation where five records on the same
individual appear. Each record is documented, but, as one
compares them, variations in the birthdates exist. (Perhaps
the occurrence of multiple records underscores the need for
the availability of a "registry" file in order to minimize
duplication of the researchers' efforts.) The example given
represents actual data. The DIALTWIG search used in this
scenario is displayed in figure 2.

Selecting on HARRISON, JOSEPHINE ASENATH as the name of
record, five postings result. (DIALTWIG creates a separate
"set" for each usage of the select command, S. In the
example, "S1" is the name automatically assigned to the set
and the one by which it may be referenced. Subsequent
"selects" will generate sets S2, S3, etc.) Displaying the
results under format "4" which posts the birth place,
birthdate, spouse's name, father's and mother's names (if
available) one observes that the birthplace and spouse is
common to all records. The father's name appears in three of
the records and the mother's name in two. All of the five
versions are very likely variations on the same person.

Next additional sets are created by selecting each of the three birth dates, in turn, and combining them with the first retrieved set, S1, thus isolating them so that their sources may be compared. Displaying the results under format "3", which posts each record's source documentation, one observes that the source existing more closely in time to the birthdate is the one for the third record in S2.[3] The other sources for the birth date were ones generated at the time of marriage (TIB),[4] at the time spiritual direction was sought later in life (Patriarchal blessing), or at locations where the individual resided during later periods of her life.

The full record, corresponding to the third record of S2, is displayed using format "5". While this record may have the most accurate birth date, other important information about the father's and mother's name is not present. Inspection of the fields within the other records together with their accompanying sources would permit the assemblage, online, of the most complete and the most accurate record for Josephine Asenath Harrison.

The main point we are trying to illustrate is that for each unit record the MARGEDOS communication format allows one to identify from which sources (if any) the data are derived and to make decisions, online, regarding its reliability. In addition it provides the capability to deal with duplicate records on the same individual--an issue that cannot be ignored.[5]

A NATIONAL STANDARD

The development of the MARC format has an interesting history. It has become a standard for bibliographic records, yet it was not intended, by any directive of the library, to

3. The range of dates on the films was obtained from the Register of Genealogical Society Call Numbers, Vol. II, A Companion to Genealogical Records of Utah, compiled by Laureen Jaussi and Gloria D. Chaston, Provo, Utah : The Genealogy Tree.

4. TIB stands for Temple Records Index Bureau, a registry of marriages performed in the temples of The Church of Jesus Christ of Latter-day Saints.

5. If one may draw another comparison between the genealogist's world and the librarian's world then provision should be made to preserve variations among duplicate records. One need only to inspect one of the shared cataloging systems (e.g.,RLIN) and observe the many variations in "holding's information" and accuracy of data which is being preserved for each bibliographic entry with respect to each library.

```
              File 3:  GENEALOGY DATA BASE
                Set Items Description
              --- --- --------------
? S HARRISON, JOSEPHINE ASENATH/NA
                 S1    5 HARRISON, JOSEPHINE ASENATH/NA
? T1/4/1-5
 1/4/1
BP Ogden, Weber, Utah
BD 12 Dec 1890
MS White, David John
FA Harrison, Joseph J.
MO Tillotson, Elizabeth A.


 1/4/2                         Code        Field Name
BP Ogden, Weber, Utah
BD 12 Dec 1890                 AN          Accession No.
MS White, David John           NA          Name
FA Harrison, Joseph J.         GD          Gender
MO Tillotson, Elizabeth A.     BP          Birthplace
                               BD          Birth Date
 1/4/3                         ZD          Baptismal Date
BP Ogden, Weber, Utah          DP          Death Place
BD 12 Dec 1891                 DD          Death Date
MS White, David John           MP          Marriage Place
FA Harrison, Joseph J.         MD          Marriage Date
                               MS          Spouse Name
 1/4/4                         SB          Source, Birth
BP Ogden, Weber, Utah          SZ          Source, Baptism
BD 2 Dec 1891                  SD          Source, Death
MS White, David John           SM          Source, Marriage
                               SP          Source, Parents
 1/4/5
BP Ogden, Weber, Utah
BD 12 Dec 1890
MS White, David John

? S BD=12 DEC 1890 AND S1
                3 BD=12 DEC 1890
        S2      3 BD=12 DEC 1890 AND S1
? S BD=12 DEC 1891 AND S1
                1 BD=12 DEC 1891
        S3      1 BD=12 DEC 1891 AND S1
? S BD=2 DEC 1891 AND S1
                1 BD=2 DEC 1891
        S4      1 BD=2 DEC 1891 AND S1

? T2/3/1-3
 2/3/1
SB LDS TIB SL#300 DLVG p. 9
SZ LDS TIB SL#300 DLVG p. 9
```

Fig. 2. A DIALTWIG Search

SD Headstone-Ogden, UT Cemetery
SM LDS SLG REC #186207 Oct 1905--
SP LDS TIB SL#300 DLVG p. 9
SP LDS TIB SL#300 DLVG p. 9

2/3/2
SB LDS Pat Bl #273 27 Nov 1917 Ogden, UT
SD FAM REC by J.J. HARRISON, father
SM Mar Application, Weber County, UT 8 Sep 1908
SP LDS Pat Bl #273 27 Nov 1917 Ogden, UT

2/3/3
SB LDS MEM REC OGDEN 4th WARD, #26230 1877--1918
SZ LDS MEM REC OGDEN 4th WARD, #26230 1877--1918
SD Obit notice, Ogden Standard Examiner 13 Mar 1921
SM LDS MEM REC OGDEN 4th WARD, #26230 1877--1918

? T3/3
 3/3/1
SB LDS Kanesville MEM REC #26064 1906--1933
SZ LDS Kanesville MEM REC #26064 1906--1933
SD FAM REC by J.J. HARRISON, father
SM LDS Kanesville MEM REC #26064 1906--1933
SP Mar Application, Weber County, UT 8 Sep 1908

? T4/3
 4/3/1
SB LDS MEM REC Ogden 11th Ward #26252 1913--1941
SZ LDS MEM REC Ogden 11th Ward #26252 1913--1941
SD LDS MEM REC Ogden 11th Ward #26252 1913--1941
SM Mar Certificate, #4198 Salt Lake County, UT

? T2/5/3
 2/5/3
AN 85AAAA
NA Harrison, Josephine Asenath
GD F
BP Ogden, Weber, Utah
BD 12 Dec 1890
ZD 17 Sep 1899
DP Ogden, Weber, Utah
DD 11 Mar 1921
MP Salt Lake City, Salt Lake, Utah
MD 9 Sep 1908
MS White, David John
SB LDS MEM REC OGDEN 4th WARD, #26230 1877--1918
SZ LDS MEM REC OGDEN 4th WARD, #26230 1877--1918
SD Obit notice, Ogden Standard Examiner 13 Mar 1921
SM LDS MEM REC OGDEN 4th WARD, #26230 1877--1918

? Logoff

Fig. 2 continued.

be a national standard. In the 1960s when networking and
technology for libraries were just beginning, the approach
was adopted that programs should be built from the ground up,
based on local and immediate needs rather than a plan
constructed around the "ideal system." MARC's development
was based on practical considerations. The Library of
Congress took the view that its role was to develop the MARC
formats as a means of providing some standardization and to
provide general direction to library growth and development.
How libraries elected to use the formats and tapes was up to
them. This encouraged experimentation and various uses by
numerous institutions. Those circumstances led to the
emergence, in an unplanned fashion, of library networks and a
"standard" communication format.[6]

The data contained in most present-day information
systems has a half-life--meaning that it will someday be
purged. Genealogical data, on the other hand, does not
become obsolete with time. In fact, even old records tend to
have more information added to them as time progresses.
Also, as interest in genealogical research continues to
increase more duplication is likely to occur. Automated
methods are needed to resolve these problems in a
cost/effective manner. The forecast is simple. Massive
genealogical data bases will continue to be developed--more
so than those of which we are presently aware.

The Library of Congress has given us a viable pattern
to follow. A similar approach is now needed for computer
processing of genealogical records. There should be a
genealogical communication format--such as
MARGEDOS--defined, used, and improved, if necessary. In
addition, an organization is needed to shepherd this
activity. Perhaps a low profile, such as the Library of
Congress used, is necessary. Regardless of how it is
done, a central agency is needed to initiate a
communication standard and to monitor its development.
Logically, the Utah Genealogical Society would seem to be
a good choice because of their available resources.
However, the major amount of genealogical research in this
country comes from non-Utah sources, so any communication
format proposed, to be successful, would need the full
collaborative support of these organizations.

---

    6. Norman D. Stevens, "Library Networks and Resource
Sharing in the United States: An Historical and
Philosophical Overview," Journal of the American Society
for Information Science 31 (Nov. 1980): 402-12.

GEDCOM: A Format for Genealogical Communications

Robert D. Foster

During the next 45 minutes I will be telling you about some of the things The Church of Jesus Christ of Latter-day Saints has done and is doing to enhance genealogical research.

First, I'll spend just a few minutes explaining why the Church is interested in genealogy and some of what we have done to support genealogical research. I will also tell you about some of the Church's plans for the future regarding genealogy. Following this brief, broad picture I will focus on one particular computer based piece of that plan, the Personal Ancestral File. Finally, I'll concentrate on the GEDCOM: what it is and how it works.

But first, the beginning. Why our involvement in genealogy? It may seem strange to many people that a religion is so deeply involved in genealogy. I assure you it is not a fad. Nor is it simply because many Church members pursue genealogy as a hobby. The Church had a vital interest in helping its members identify their deceased ancestors. We are also encouraged to keep close family ties with living relatives through the establishment of family organizations and holding of family reunions, to write our personal history, and to keep a journal of our lives for our posterity.

This interest in past, present, and future family is rooted in our beliefs concerning the importance of and eternal nature of the family. We believe that family relations can endure beyond this life. However, in order for this to occur certain religious ordinances are performed in the temples of the Church. These ordinances make is necessary for living Church members to identify their deceased ancestors, whose names are sent to a temple where the ordinances are performed for them by living proxies.

To assist members in searching out and identifying their deceased ancestors, the Church has established a genealogical library in Salt Lake City, Utah, with about 550 branch libraries throughout the world. While this library system was established especially for Church members, everyone, regardless of religious affiliation, is welcome to use any of the available facilities. The Church is very active in identifying and obtaining copies of genealogical records from around the world. These ever expanding holdings contain a wide variety of civil, religious, and other records of value to the genealogists.

In addition to the holdings, the library has an experienced staff of specialists ready to assist the researcher in a number of ways. They can give advice on how to conduct research for a specific area, help understand what something cryptic means, and so on. This help is available either in person at the library in Salt Lake City or by correspondence.

All of the research materials in the library has are either on paper or film. No computerized information is directly available to researchers. Only microfiche indexes of computerized material are available for research. These indexes refer the researcher to microfilms of the source material the computerized data came from.

The Church has long recognized the potential value of computers in genealogical research. The Church's first computerization projects began in the 1960s. As proven technology becomes practical, the Church takes advantage of it where appropriate. Plans have been prepared and are being followed to computerize as much research material as practical and to provide the means for researchers to search this computerized data far more efficiently and quickly than is possible with paper and film based data. Let me caution that this capability will not be available soon. However, when it is available, initially only researchers who can come to the library in Salt Lake City will be able to have access to these computerized data files. But we can now see the day when a genealogical researcher with a home computer will be able to sit at home and have access to these computerized files.

As a first step toward helping genealogists become familiar with using a computer for genealogy, the Church has produced a computer program for the IBM personal computer. This program is called the Personal Ancestral File. Version 1.0 of the Personal Ancestral File contains two components, the Lineage-linked Subsystem and the Data Sort Utility.

The most popular component is the Lineage-linked Subsystem. This component stores information about individual members of a family and then links those individuals together into family groups and pedigrees. It allows you to examine the information on the computer screen and to produce a variety of printed reports, including family group records and pedigree charts.

The second component is the Data Sort Utility. This program allows you to enter and store large volumes of event-oriented research data and associated source references in the computer. By event-oriented, I mean an event such as a birth, marriage, death, etc., and the names of the individuals, the date, the place, and other information associated with that event. It also provides a variety of ways to search through and sort that data.

A new release of the Personal Ancestral File has been under development. This version (Version 2.0) will not only operate on the IBM PC, but on the Apple II family of computers, on selected computers that use the CP/M operating system, such as Kaypro, and on Radio Shack computers with MS DOS or CP/M. In addition, we are working on putting the Personal Ancestral File on the Commodore 64 computer. We expect to be providing versions for other popular computers in the future.

Version 2.0 not only has improved and enhanced Lineage-linked (now called the Family Records Program) and Data Sort Utility (now called Research Data Filer) components, it has a new component as well: the Communication Subsystem.

The Communication Subsystem allows you to identify a portion of your lineage-linked data base that you want to make a copy of. You may designate an individual, a family group, or an ascending or descending pedigree line. The data you designate is copied from the data base into a GEDCOM formatted field, which I will define in a moment. The data in this GEDCOM file may be put into another of your own family records data bases or it may be sent to another person who can put it into his own family records data base. The Communication Subsystem puts data from a GEDCOM file into a family records data base, but does not link that data with data already in the data base. One must use the Family Records Program facilities to establish any such ties.

Distribution of Personal Ancestral File Version 1.0 began in April 1984. Release 2.0 is now being prepared.

Distribution should begin later of this year. You may find out when it is available by calling the Ancestral File Operations Unit at 801-531-2584.

Because of the data extracted by the Communication Subsystem is in GEDCOM format, it may be shared with a person who uses a genealogy program other than Personal Ancestral File, if that other genealogy program supports GEDCOM files. The file may be transmitted to another person on tape, diskette, or via telecommunications.

And all of this brings us to a discussion of the GEDCOM format, or, in its full name, a Genealogical Data Communications format.

For this discussion I will first explain what the GEDCOM format is, then I will show an example of how data in a typical computer format looks compared with how it looks in GEDCOM format.

The GEDCOM format is used within a computer program to represent genealogical data in such a way that it can easily be shared by one computer program or they may be different programs. It is only intended for passing the data between systems. It is not intended for nor is it good for storing data in the computer so that it can be easily searched and manipulated. Since GEDCOM is just a format, it does not address what the data is, only how it looks. As I mentioned a moment ago GEDCOM is independent of the media. GEDCOM data may be passed via telecommunications, on disk or tape, or even on paper.

GEDCOM doesn't even care what character set is used. It is permissible to use a character set that incorporates European or Scandinavian characters or even a foreign alphabet such as the Hebrew, Greek, or Cyrillic alphabet. Actually, it is more accurate to say that GEDCOM doesn't care as long as two conditions are met. First, the parties sharing the data both know and agree what alphabet is used. Second, that characters are identified for specific GEDCOM use. Most of these special characters may also be used in data as long as some rules are followed. (What these special characters are used for will be discussed in just a moment.)

Figure 1 shows how the data from our discussion is organized. We have data for individuals in one file, information that ties those individuals together into another file, and a third file which contains bibliographic source citation data.

One record in the individual file contains this information: key number (4 digits), name (20 characters), birthdate (11 characters; 2 for day, 3 for month, and 4 for year), marriage pointer (4 digits), and a source pointer (4 digits). (I've kept the amount of information in figure 2 short to avoid getting lost in a mass of data.

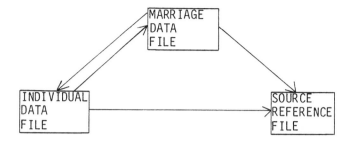

Fig. 1. Typical File Structure

One record in the marriage file contains: key number (4 digits), wife pointer (4 digits), and a source pointer (4 digits).

One record in the source reference file contains: key number (4 digits), document name (30 characters), and a reference number (6 characters).

Figure 3 shows the actual data we will be working with in our example.

I have limited it to just two individuals, one marriage, and three sources for the sake of clarity. It is not intended to be representative of all the data a

KEY	NAME		BIRTHDATE			MARR PTR	SRCE PTR
			DY	MON	YEAR	PTR	PTR
(4)	(20)		2	(3)	(4)	(4)	(4)

KEY	MARR DATE			HUSB PTR	WIFE PTR	SRCE PTR
	DY	MON	YEAR	PTR	PTR	PTR
(4)	2	(3)	(4)	(4)	(4)	(4)

KEY	DOCUMENT NAME	REF NO
(4)	(30)	(6)

Fig. 2. Sample records in individual file (top), marriage file (middle), and source reference file (bottom)

```
0001JOHN JAMES DOE      02FEB194000050007
0002MARY ELIZABETH BROWN13SEP194300050008
```

```
000526NOV1965000100020009
```

```
0007BIRTH CERTIFICATE OF UTAH       BC0019
0008BIRTH CERTIFICATE OF OREGON     BC0028
0009MARRIAGE CERTIFICATE OF UTAH    MC0010
```

Fig. 3 Example of information showing birth and marriage dates and sources of verification

good genealogical data management system should have. It is only intended to show an example of how GEDCOM works. In actual practice virtually any type and amount of data may be represented in a GEDCOM data file.

You can see how the pointers link information in one record to information in other records. By looking at the birthdate you can also see how information can be (and often is) subdivided into smaller pieces.

I also want to point out that there is nothing in the data itself that says what it is. The burden is on the computer program to read and interpret the data correctly. If the program is not written correctly, it will not be able to interpret the data correctly. This situation is not a unique future of this example. This situation is nearly universal in computerized data storage.

Now let's put this data into the GEDCOM format.

The conversion from the typical data format to the GEDCOM format is done by separating each records being converted into single fields. Each field, or piece of data, is given a label telling what the data is, indicators telling how this piece relates to the other pieces of data around it, and a way of telling how big this record is.

Let's build one GEDCOM record first. We'll use the name from the first individual record. First, we put a label, or TAG, in front of the name. Let's use the TAG NAME. Let me say here that it is essential that the systems which will be sharing this data both know and agree what TAGs are used and how they are used. For example, in Personal Ancestral File we have prepared a dictionary of all the TAGs we use and how we use them. We use only two character TAGs in Personal Ancestral File, but GEDCOM doesn't care how long the TAG is as long as it is just one word. The reason for this is that a space tells where the TAG ends and the data begins.

In front of the TAG we put a single digit that we call a LEVEL. The LEVEL tells how this piece of data is related to other pieces it is closely associated with. In this example the LEVEL is 1. What this means will become clearer in just a moment when we convert all the other fields in this individual record.

If the piece of data has a separate access key directly assigned to it, the key value is put in between the LEVEL and the TAG. We call this an XR-OBJECT, short for cross-reference object. The key value is enclosed in AT signs (@). The AT sign is one of those special characters I mentioned earlier. This key value may include any character, numeric digit, alphabetic character, and even special characters such as a period, comma, etc. It can include any character except an AT sign. Of course, if this piece of data has no key value then there will be no XR-OBJECT in the GEDCOM record. In our example here, the name field in the source record has no key assigned to it, so there is no XR-OBJECT in this GEDCOM record. But we will see an example of it shortly.

Finally, to complete our GEDCOM record we need to show how big this record is. That can be done in one of two ways. Whichever way it is done, the same way must be used throughout this set of GEDCOM records.

The first way is to attach another field that says how many characters there are in the GEDCOM record. This includes not only the data itself but the TAG, LEVEL, and XR-OBJECT (if there is one) as well. Then we we can just count characters and know when we counted that many we would be at the end of this GEDCOM record and at the beginning of the next. If we used that method in our example here we would proceed the LEVEL with a count of 20. If we count 20 characters, we do come to the end of this GEDCOM record.

However, in our example we are going to use the other method. A TERMINATOR. This is another special character sequence. It signals the end of the GEDCOM record. It cannot be used anywhere else in this set of records. If I use a terminator or pound sign (#) in our example, my computer program that was reading this record would just look at characters until it saw the pound sign. Then it would know it was at the end of one record and ready to begin reading the next.

In the Personal Ancestral File we use the TERMINATOR method, only our TERMINATOR is a carriage return or a carriage return followed by a line feed. But since you can't easily show those characters on paper, I'm going to use the pound sign for our example. I can't recommend it for real use though, since whatever character is chosen cannot ever occur as data.

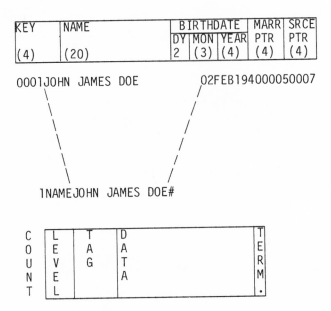

Fig. 4.   A GEDCOM Record

Figure 4 is an example of GEDCOM record. Now let's see what the whole record from our individual file looks like when it's converted to GEDCOM.

This is how it will really look:

    0@1@INDIVIDUAL#1NAME JOHN JAMES DOE#1BIRTHDATE#2DAY
    2#2MONTH FEB#2YEAR 1941#1 MARRIAGE @5@#1SOURCE @7@#.

But since this is hard to read, I took the liberty of putting each GEDCOM record on a separate line. That's one of the main reasons we use the carriage return and line feed for the TERMINATOR in the Personal Ancestral File. Whenever GEDCOM data is printed out, it's easier to read. (See figure 5.)

First, note that some GEDCOM records don't have any data. You will also see that there is no data in the individual record that corresponds to those TAGs. However, there are labels in the individual record that correspond to those TAGS. See how the "Individual" TAG corresponds to the "Individual" label for the record itself. Further see how the "Birthdate" TAG corresponds to the "Birthdate" label, even though the birthdate data itself has been subdivided. When you see a GEDCOM record that has no data this normally means that subsequent GEDCOM records contain a finer breakdown of data.

```
KEY  |NAME                    |BIRTHDATE|MARR|SRCE|
001JOHN  JAMES DOE          02FEB194000050007
```

```
0@1@INDIVIDUAL#
1NAME JOHN JAMES DOE#
1BIRTHDATE#
2DAY 2#
2MONTH FEB#
2YEAR 1941#
1MARRIAGE @5@#
1SOURCE @7@#
```

Fig. 5. A GEDCOM Data File

See how the LEVEL supports that breakdown and shows
when the breakdown stops. The rule is that all lower
level GEDCOM records (those whose LEVEL value is larger)
immediately after a higher level GEDCOM record contain
data that pertains to that pertains to that higher level
GEDCOM record. For example, the Day, Month, and Year
GEDCOM records at LEVEL 2 contain data that pertains to
the Birthdate GEDCOM record at LEVEL 1 immediately
preceeding them. The Marriage Pointer record following
the Year record is at LEVEL. This shows that Marriage
Pointer contains the same level of information as
Birthdate.

Similarly, every GEDCOM record following the LEVEL 0
Individual GEDCOM record contains information that
pertains to one individual.

LEVEL can be any sequence of characters as long as
they are in an ascending in sequence. In our example we
use numbers but letters, such as A thru C, would be just
as valid. What characters are used can vary with the
character set used.

As we add the GEDCOM records with data for the second
person in our Individual File you can see in figure 6 that
it starts over at LEVEL 0.

```
0002MARY ELIZABETH BROWN13SEP194300050008
```

```
0@2@INDIVIDUAL#
1NAME MARY ELIZABETH BROWN#
1BIRTHDATE#
2DAY 13#
2MONTH SEP#
2YEAR 1943#
1MARRIAGE @5@#
1SOURCE @8@#
```

Fig. 6. Building an individual file

Finally, you see that GEDCOM records built with data from pointer fields in the individual record now contain those pointer values enclosed in AT signs. When a pointer value precedes the TAG we call it an XR-OBJECT. In that position it denoted a key or flag that allows it to be referenced from other places. When a pointer value follows a TAG we call it an XR-POINTER. In this position it now points to something else being referenced.

As we add the converted data from the Family and Source Files you can see in figure 7 how the pointers do in fact point to records in those other files and vice versa.

This set of GEDCOM records make up a GEDCOM file. This whole file would be transmitted as a single unit. The receiver would have to interpret the data and put it into this own data files. Those files may have the same structure as the sender's files or they may be different.

It is important to understand that one computer system cannot start preparing GEDCOM files without first coming to an agreement with other systems who will be organized (i.e., by individual, by family group, etc.); what TAGS will be used; any restrictions on where TAGs can be used (such as what LEVEL or subordinate to or in association with another TAG, etc.); whether length or TERMINATOR will be used; what the TERMINATOR is, if used; whether cross-reference objects and pointers will be used and where; what character set is used; and any other issues and characteristics and restrictions that may be appropriate.

The key thing to remember is that GEDCOM does not tell you everything. It only established a foundation and framework that needs to be filled out. As we gain experience with GEDCOM we will reach agreements on these other issues. But to attempt to include these other things into GEDCOM right now would be premature because we just haven't done enough work yet to be able to say for sure what else ought to be established as a standard. That can only happen after much more thought, discussion, and experience. Our implementation of GEDCOM in the Personal Ancestral File is intended to provide that experience.

We have in the past and are currently discussing GEDCOM and its implications with several interested parties in the genealogical community. Some of them are developers of other genealogy management programs for home computers.

In closing, let me briefly state what we feel are the benefits of GEDCOM.

First, the context of the data is preserved. This includes how pieces fit together with other pieces around them. Second, since GEDCOM data is independent of any

```
KEY|MARR DATE|HUSB|WIFE|SRCE|
000526NOV1965000100020009
```

```
KEY|DOCUMENT NAME                    |REF NO|
0007BIRTH CERTIFICATE OF UTAH      BC0014
0008BIRTH CERTIFICATE OF OREGON    BC0028
0009MARRIAGE CERTIFICATE OF UTAH MC0010
```

```
0@5@MARRIAGE#
1MARRIAGE_DATE#
2DAY 26#
2MONTH NOV#
2YEAR 1965#
1HUSBAND @1@#
1WIFE @2@#
1SOURCE @9@#
0@7@SOURCE#
1DOCUMENT BIRTH CERTIFICATE OF UTAH
1REFERENCE BC0014#
0@8@SOURCE#
1DOCUMENT BIRTH CERTIFICATE OF OREGON#
1REFERENCE BC0028#
0@9@SOURCE#
1DOCUMENT MARRIAGE CERTIFICATE OF UTAH#
1REFERENCE MC0010#
```

Fig. 7. A GEDCOM file

internal computer storage format, a user of one program
can share genealogical data with a user of a different
program.   Third, because GEDCOM data is not position
dependent it is easy to add new data items and to ignore
ones that are of no interest to your system.   Fourth, any
of a variety of media can be used to transfer GEDCOM data
from one user to another.

In the end, our ultimate goal is to make it easier and
simpler to pass data from one computer system to another.
As we do so, we increase the resources available to the
genealogist and make his time spent in genealogy more
effective and rewarding.

The Use of Online Searching in Genealogy

John C. Cosgriff, Jr.

As should be evident by now, we have entered into the information age, and online environments are becoming more and more common in libraries and other information centers.

Public agencies and commercial vendors are offering online data bases containing great varieties of information which are retrievable in most cases from home or library or office simply by using a low-cost personal computer or terminal, a modem, and a telephone or telephone jack.

Although most of these data bases at the present time are designed to service fields in the economic mainstream: law, medicine, engineering, science, and business, some existing data bases do have value to genealogists and local historians. Some of these are: Biography Master Index, America: History and Life, Historical Abstracts, Dissertation Abstracts Online, Marquis Who's Who, and Social Scisearch.

ADVANTAGES

What advantages do online data bases have over conventional printed indexes? There are at least four. Everybody is probably well acquainted already with the obvious and important advantages of speed and accuracy which the use of computer makes possible, and so, as important as these are, I will only mention them in passing. There are at least two other important advantages associated with online searching techniques: access points and precision.

Computerized data bases generally offer many more access points than do conventional indexes and abstracts. This, of course, greatly increases searching options and effectiveness. For example, consider using the printed versions of Marquis Who's Whos versus the online version. Using the printed version we can only access the names of the subjects. These are listed alphabetically. Using the online version, however, we cannot only access the names of the subjects, but also the maiden names of wives or mothers of the subjects, as well as their fathers, children, any other in-laws named, the name of their hometown, or college from which they graduated.

When I looked up my own name of Cosgriff online, for example, I was able to find besides those few men surnamed Cosgriff who were mentioned in this source, women whose maiden names were Cosgriff whose husbands of entirely different surnames were listed. Thus we are able to retrieve references online which are unavailable manually. For example, we can search for all women with a particular maiden name; all who are born in a particular year; all who went to a certain university; all who married to a person of a particular surname; all who worked for a particular company; all who served in a particular military unit, and so on and on. None of these could be searched for effectively in any other way than online. Notice in figure 1 how the maiden names of spouses can be retrieved.

With this example, I searched for the surname Cosgriff. The first set contained three entries, of which the second entry would be very difficult to retrieve in the printed versions.

Note that with the above data base we obtain different pieces of information with the various format options: format 1 gives only the Dialog accession number, format 2 gives professional data about the person, format 3 (the one I used) gives personal data, format 5 gives the full record except the street address, format 6 gives brief reference data, format 7 gives educational data, format 8 gives achievements/affiliation data, and format 9 gives the full record. We are charged more for the full record.

A fourth advantage offered by online searching is precision. Online we can use Boolean logic to make our searching more precise. Let's say we are interested in the city of Philadelphia. We want information on Philadelphia for the years 1805-7, and if we were searching manually for that information, we would obviously have to wade through a lot of information on Philadelphia in order to find what we are specifically

```
                    Set Items Description
                    --- ----- -----------
? s cosgriff
                      1    3 COSGRIFF
? t 1/3/1-3
1/3/1 1391559  WA43  BIOG UPDATE:  19830000
   Cosgriff, Stuart Worcester
   BORN:  May 8, 1917 Pittsfield, MA  US
   PARENTS:  Thomas F Cosgriff and Frances
             Deford Worcester Cosgriff
   SEX:  Male
   FAMILY:  married Mary Shaw, January 23, 1943;
            children Mary, Thomas, Stuart, Richard,
            Robert

1/3/2 377984  WA42  BIOG UPDATE:  19820601
   Kennedy, Quentin James
   BORN:  May 27, 1933 NYC, NY  US
   PARENTS:  John R Kennedy and Ethel Rose
             Leavy Kennedy
   SEX:  Male
   FAMILY: married Mary Elizabeth Cosgriff, September
            18, 1956; children-Quentin James, Peter E,
            Megan M, Mary Kate

1/3/3 180472  WA42  BIOG UPDATE:  19820601
   Cosgriff, Stewart
   BORN:  June, 30 1903 Salt Lake City, UT US
   PARENTS:  John B Cosgriff and Bessie
             Stewart Cosgriff
   SEX:  Male
   FAMILY:  married Katharine Dawson, December 19,
            1927; children-Katharine (Mrs James B
            Kurtz), Peter, Susan (Mrs. Gilbert A
            Mueller), Bridget (Mrs. Bridget Fisher
```

Fig. 1. Example from Marquis Who's Who: This example illustrates the ability to retrieve names unaccessible in the printed indexes

after. By searching online, we can use the Boolean operator "and," and limit our retrieval to those two search parameters, "Philadelphia" and "1805-1807." Thus, we are able to get just those entries we want pertaining to Philadelphia in those three years.

There are several of these, known as "Boolean" and "proximity" operators, which allow us to precisely narrow or broaden our search: AND, OR, NOT, and proximity operators, such as (W), (A), and (L). Also fields can be specified, such as in "/title," "/author," or "/abstract,"

which will eliminate for consideration all fields but
those which we have specified to be searched.

EXISTING ONLINE DATA BASES

Permit me to go through some searching with you to
demonstrate what is available online. I realize that
nothing is quite as dull as the other fellow's genealogy,
however, I hope you will relate the use of these data
bases to your own situations.

My challenge was to find information on the Cosgriff
family which appeared in the township of Ennismore,
Peterborough Co., Ontario, Canada in 1847, and then
scattered in both the United States and Canada. Like many
immigrant families from Ireland and elsewhere the surname
was spelled in various ways.

Ideally, we would like to find information on
Cosgriffs in Ennismore in 1847, however, it will probably
be necessary to broaden the search to include articles and
books about Cosgriffs anywhere in North America, and
information about Peterborough and Ontario as well. Also,
I was interested on information on Irish immigration and
migration in North America which might offer clues.

SURNAME SEARCHING

Let's begin by seeing what is available on Dialog's
data bases for the surname Cosgriff and a few related
spellings. A good place to begin is with the DIALINDEX
file. Once in DIALINDEX, we can specify those files we
wish to examine either by giving the files numbers or by
asking for certain categories of files, e.g., those
dealing with people or biography. (See figures 2 and 3.)

In these examples, we requested the people files, and
then searched for cosgr? (truncated to find possible
variant spellings. DIALINDEX gives us an indication that
the most productive files to search for the surnames in
question are Social Scisearch with 26 hits, Dissertation
Abstracts Online with 4 hits, Magazine Index with 39 hits,
National Newspaper Index with 33 hits, Marquis Who's Who
with 21 hits, American Men & Women of Science with 7 hits,
Biography Master Index--A-M with 199 hits, and Biography
Master Index--N-Z with 7 hits. Each of these files are
worthy of further searching. We will examine each of them
in turn.

A quick perusal of Social Scisearch (figure 4) did not
indicate any relevant material on my ancestors or their
descendants. This evaluative process should not be left

```
                    ? s files people

File7:SOCIAL SCISEARCH - 72-84/Wk50
File34:SCISEARCH - 84/Wk 48
File35:DISSERTATION ABSTRACTS ONLINE 1861 to Jan 85
File47:MAGAZINE INDEX - 1959, Mar 1973-85/JAN
File87:SCISEARCH - 81-83
File94:SCISEARCH - 78-80
File111:NATIONAL NEWSPAPER INDEX - 79-85/Jan
File186:SCISEARCH - 74-77
File234:Marquis Who s Who-82-84/Sep
File236:American Men & Women of Science 15th Ed.

                    File Items Description
                    ---- ----- -----------
? s cosgr?
                    (7)  [File 7 is Social Scisearch]
                           26 COSGR?

                    (34) [File 34 is Scisearch--1984+]
                            1 COSGR?

                    (35) [File 35 is Dissertation Abstracts]
                            4 COSGR?

                    (47) [File 47 is Magazine Index]
                           39 COSGR?

                    (87) [File 87 is Scisearch--1981 to 1983]
                            1 COSGR?

                    (94) [File 94 is Scisearch--1978 to 1980]
                            1 COSGR?

                    (111)[File 111 is National Newspaper Index]
                           35 COSGR?

                    (186)[File 186 is Scisearch--1974 to 1977]
                            3 COSGR?

                    (234) File 234 is Marquis Who's Who]
                           21 COSGR?

                    (236)[File 236 is Am. Men & Women of Sci.]
                            7 COSGR?
```

Fig. 2.   Example from DIALINDEX^{T.M.}

```
? s files biograph

File162:Career Placement Registry/Exper. Personnel/Jan
         11 1985
File163:Career Placement Registry/Student-Jan 08, 1985
File234:Marquis Who's Who-82-84/Sep
File236:American Men & Women of Science 15th Ed.
File287:Biography Master Index - - A-M
File288:Biography Master Index - - N-Z

                 File Items Description
                 ---- ----- -----------

? s cosgr?
                 (234)
                         21    COSGR?

                 (236)
                          7    COSGR?

                 (287)
                        199    COSGR?

                 (288)
                          7    COSGR?
```

Fig. 3.   Example from DIALINDEX

```
           Set Items Description
           --- ----- -----------
? s cosgr?
           1    26 COSGR?

? t 1/3/1

1/3/1 1559918 OATS ORDER#:PW794 2 REFS
  THE RULE OF LAW - DICEY, ALBERT,VENN,
  VICTORIAN JURIST - COSGROVE,RA (EN)
  DUFFY IPH
  LEHIGH UNIV/BETHLEHEM//PA/18015
  AMERICAN JOURNAL OF LEGAL HISTORY , V26,
  N4 P386-387, 1982
```

Fig. 4.   Example from Social Scisearch

to the data base. For this reason, when searching, I
prefer to receive too much and do the selecting myself
rather than trusting the indexers or the computer to do it.

Magazine Index likewise did not show any relevant
entries (figure 5).

```
        File47:MAGAZINE INDEX - 1959-Mar 1970, 1973-
                85/Feb (Copr. IAC) FMT 9 = $7.00
        [full text is $7.00 per article]
                Set Items Description
                --- ----- -----------


        ? ss cosgr?
               1      39 COSGR?
        ? t 1/8/1-39 1/8/1 1810233 DATABASE: MI File
           47 Sleepy time bunny. (book reviews)
           NAMED PEOPLE:  Cosgrove, Stephen; Reasoner,
                           Charles
           DESCRIPTORS:  books-reviews, etc.

        1/8/33 0879680 DATABASE:  MI File 47
             Gentleman Jack gets back.  (surprising vote
             in lackluster campaign)
             NAMED PEOPLE:  Lynch, John; Cosgrave, Liam
             DESCRIPTORS:  elections-Ireland
```

Fig. 5. Example from Magazine Index

National Newspaper Index picked up one Cosgriff about
whom I would like to find out more. Also, it picked up
obituaries which may prove valuable (figure 6).

American Men & Women of Science picked up another
possible relative (figure 7). Unfortunately, unlike
Marquis Who's Who, it does not list the names of spouses,
children, or parents.

Biography Master Index picked up so much that I
limited it to the spelling, Cosgriff, in order to keep the
cost down (figure 8). Unfortunately, this fine file is not
inexpensive. The 23 types cost $8.05 (.35 each).

Although the last half of the alphabet in Biography
Master Index revealed nothing of relevance (figure 9),
it is another good example of the accesssing power of an
online data base. Now how it picks up the middle names
Unfortunately, the reference given by this index is not to
the source document up to other indexes, such as Biography
Index. But, it picked up far more relevant surnames than
any other files.

```
File111:NATIONAL NEWSPAPER INDEX - 79-85/FEB
        (Copr. IAC)
        Set Items Description
        --- ----- -----------
? ss cosgr?
             1    33 COSGR?

? t 1/3/29-33

1/3/29 0102157   DATABASE:  NNI File 111
   Rev. Raymond R. Cosgrove. (obituary)
   New York Times v 128  Section A pA14 Aug 1
                   1979
   CODEN:  NYTIA
   col 6    002 col in.
   EDITION:  Wed


1/3/30  0321444   DATABASE:  NNI File 111
   Ideal Basic Industries Inc. (personnel
   change) Wall Street Journal  v104  Section 2
   p29(W) p29(E)  March 9 1981
   CODEN:  WSJOAF
   col 2  001  col in.
   EDITION:  Mon
   GEOGRAPHIC LOCATION:  Denver
   NAMED PEOPLE:  Pindar, Herbert C.-selection
     and appointments
   Cosgriff, Stewart C.-retirement
   DESCRIPTORS: Ideal Basic Industries Inc.-
     officials and employees
```

Fig. 6. Example from National Newspaper Index

Since there were no hits for Cosgriff, I tried the
truncated form, Cosgr? I have attempted to demonstrate
the value of some of data bases in searching for the
surnames. Granted, the cost is high for some of our
genealogists, yet the ability to access middle names and
maiden names make them powerful tools. Having finished
searching for the surname in question, we next turn our
attention to places and events.

PLACES AND EVENTS

For most online searching for genealogical
information, we would begin searching for information on
the geographical areas in which the ancestors in question

```
              Set Items Description
              ---  -----  -----------

    ? s cosgr?
              1      7 COSGR?

    ? t 1/8/1-7

    1/8/7 0020149
        Cosgriff, John W, Jr.
        Discipline:  PALEONTOLOGY (06006000)
        Subject Specialty:  VERTEBRATE PALEONTOLOGY
        Born: Denver, Colo, Nov 10, 31  Married 57
    No. of Children:  2
        Education:  Univ Ariz  BA 53; Univ Calif
    Berkeley MA 60 PhD(paleont) 63
        Professional Experience:  Sr res fel paleont
    Univ  Tasmania 64-67; PROF BIOL WAYNE STATE
    UNIV 67 to present
        Concurrent Positions:  Res assoc geol Univ
    Tasmania 75 to present
        Memberships:  AAAS; Soc Vert Paleont;
    Paleont Soc
        Research:  Mesozoic vertebrate faunas of
    Australia, Antarctica, Africa and North
        America Category:  Academic
        Address:  Dept of Biol Col of Lib Arts,
    Wayne State Univ. Detroit, MI   48202
```

Fig. 7. Example from American Men & Women of Science

resided. As in any search, it is best to begin searching
for the specific terms and then broadening the search if
too little is found. In this case, however, Ennismore
being a township rather than a town or a city, I chose to
begin with the county. Once again I started with the
DIALINDEX file. Of the DIALINDEX file groupings, the two
that looked the most promising were humanities group and
the books group. So entering the DIALINDEX file, I asked
for the humanities group as shown in the following
example. I then searched for Peterborough and Ontario in
both file groups (figure 10).

From examining the hits in DIALINDEX, it appeared that
the best data bases to try were Social Scisearch with 415
hits, America: History & Life with 9 hits, Art Modern with
5 hits, REMARC-pre-1900 with 1 hit, REMARC-1900-1939 with
1 hit, REMARC-1940-1959 with 1 hit, and LC MARC with 11
hits (figure 11).

There are some problems with Social Scisearch which
are difficult to solve online. It is a very useful file
when you are looking for articles which have cited a paper

```
                Set Items Description
                --- ----- -----------

        ? s cosgriff
                1    21 COSGRIFF
        ? t 1/3/1-21
        1/3/1
         1453020
         Miller, Kit Cosgriff 1/3/2
         444018
         Cosgriff, Walter Everett    1914-1961;

        ? t 1/5/1-2

        1/5/1
         1453020
         Miller, Kit Cosgriff
         International Who's Who in Poetry, 5th ed,
        1977; Pseudonyms and Pen Names of Included
        Authors", (IntWWP 77X)

        1/5/2
         444018
         Cosgriff, Walter Everett  1914-1961;
         Biography Index,Vol. 4, (BioIn 4)
         Biography Index,Vol. 6, (BioIn 6)
         National Cyclopaedia of American Biography,
        Vol. 46, (NatCAB 46)
         Who Was Who in America,Vol. 4, 1961-1968,
        (WhAm 4)
```

Fig. 8.   Example from Biography Master Index--A-M

```
                Set Items Description
                --- ----- -----------

        ? s cosgriff
                1     0 COSGRIFF

        ? s cosgr?
                2     7 COSGR?

        ? t 2/3/1-7
        2/3/1
            720376
            Weir, Hugh Cosgro  1884-1934;

        2/3/2
            534399
            Suehr, Cecile Frances Cosgrove  1898;
```

Fig. 9.   Example from Biography Master Index--N-Z

```
                  ? s files humanit

          File7 SOCIAL SCISEARCH - 72-84/Wk50
          File38 America: History & Life - 63-84/ Iss21A2
          File39 Historical Abstracts - 73-84/ Iss35B2
          File56 Art Modern - 1974 thru Jun 1984
          File57 Philosopher s Index - 40-83/Oct
          File71 MLA INTERNATIONAL BIBLIOGRAPHY -
      1970 THRU 1983
          File97 RILM - 71-78/Aug


              File Items Description
              ---- ----- -----------
      ? s peterborough and ontario
              (7)    [Social Scisearch]
                     472 PETERBOROUGH
                 34591 ONTARIO
                   415 1 AND 2

              (38)   [America: History & Life]
                      15 PETERBOROUGH
                    1794 ONTARIO
                       9 1 AND 2

              (39)   [Historical Abstracts]
                       6 PETERBOROUGH
                      14 ONTARIO
                       0 1 AND 2

              (56)   [Art Bibliographies Modern]
                       8 PETERBOROUGH
                     342 ONTARIO
                       5 1 AND 2

              (57)   [Philosopher's Index]
                       0 PETERBOROUGH
                      11 ONTARIO
                       0 1 AND 2

              (71)   [MLA Bibliography]
                      27 PETERBOROUGH
                     115 ONTARIO
                       0 1 AND 2

              (97)   [RILM Abstracts]
                       0 PETERBOROUGH
                      20 ONTARIO
                       0 1 AND 2
```

Fig. 10.   Example from DIALINDEX

```
? s files books

File421:REMARC - pre-1900 (to Z) 1984/Oct
File422:REMARC - 1900-1939 (to Z) 1984/Oct
File423:REMARC - 1940-1959 (to Z) 1984/Oct
File424:REMARC - 1960-1969 (to Z) 1984/Oct
File425:REMARC - 1970-1980 (to Z) 1984/Oct
File426:LC MARC - 68-84/JUN File470:BOOKS
IN PRINT - 1490-1984/Sep File471:Wiley
Catalog/Online - Apr 84
   File Items Description
   ---- ----- -----------
? s peterborough and ontario
   (421)  [REMARC pre-1900]
             30 PETERBOROUGH
           372 ONTARIO
             1 PETERBOROUGH AND ONTARIO
   (422)  [REMARC 1900-1939]
             25 PETERBOROUGH
           508 ONTARIO
             1 PETERBOROUGH AND ONTARIO
   (423)  [REMARC 1940-1959]
             14 PETERBOROUGH
           163 ONTARIO
             1 PETERBOROUGH AND ONTARIO
   (424)  [REMARC 1960-1969]
              5 PETERBOROUGH
           151 ONTARIO
              0 PETERBOROUGH AND ONTARIO
   (425)  [REMARC 1970-1980]
              1 PETERBOROUGH
             39 ONTARIO
              0 PETERBOROUGH AND ONTARIO
   (426)  [LC MARC 1968-last update]
             64 PETERBOROUGH
          3714 ONTARIO
             11 PETERBOROUGH AND ONTARIO
   (470)  [Books in Print 1490-last
             update]
             18 PETERBOROUGH
           180 ONTARIO
              0 PETERBOROUGH AND ONTARIO
   (471)  [Wiley Catalog/Online]
              0 PETERBOROUGH
              6 ONTARIO
              0 PETERBOROUGH AND ONTARIO
```

Fig. 11.   Example from DIALINDEX

of known relevancy to your research. In doing subject
searching, however, do not make the same mistake I did. I
learned the expensive way that what you retrieve is not
always what you thought you retrieved.

Search terms without some type of limiting prefix or
suffix give you information from all or many fields. For
some searches where you find few hits this is fine. But,
in the case of many hits, the number needs to be reduced
to eliminate irrelevant articles and yet ensure that those
you want are retrieved. With Social Scisearch, using
terms with no prefix or suffix limiters retrieves both
title words and corporate source terms. I forgot that
there is a university, Trent University, in Peterborough,
Ontario. Consequently, I picked up every article written
by Trent University professors in the journals covered by
this index. Figure 12 illustrates my error, and how I was
able to correct it by limiting the terms to the title.
Instead of the 16 hits, I now retrieved only one.

I did not get what I hoped to retrieve. However, as
you can readily perceive, limiting the search to the title
field was a step in the right direction. Another good
approach is to search the books cataloged by the Library
of Congress, which are accessible through the LC MARC and
REMARC files. This is a more powerful search through
Dialog than it would be through OCLC because Dialog offers
more access points and a more precise searching capability.

This search uncovered a gem of a book, The Holy Land,
a History of Ennismore Township, County of Peterborough,
Ontario, 1825=1975 (figure 13). This book was a direct
hit as far as I was concerned. It proved to have
information on the Cosgriff family as well as a wealth of
background information.

The example shown in figure 14 has great potential for
background information in genealogy, but unfortunately
most journals covering genealogy per se are not covered.
Nevertheless, America: History and Life is one that
should be searched.

Since there were too many hits with (irish or ireland)
and immigration, I reduced the number by requiring also
the terms (ontario or canada). This decision was based
solely on cost since some of the articles in the broader
search may have been of interest.

Note that in the search shown in figure 15 the word
immigration was too limiting. Therefore, I had the
reference from line 8 typed.

Next we plug in the names of the first authors of
relevant articles to see if we find other relevant
articles among those papers in which these have been cited
(figure 16).

```
        Set Items Description
        --- ----- -----------
? s peterborough and ontario and history
          474 PETERBOROUGH
        34591 ONTARIO
        23804 HISTORY
        1 16  PETERBOROUGH AND ONTARIO
              AND HISTORY
? t 1/3/1-16
1/3/1
1678650  OATS ORDER#:  RJ113  1  REFS
ESSAYS IN THE HISTORY OF CANADIAN LAW,
VOL 1 - FLAHERTY, DH (EN) KETTLER D
TRENT UNIV, DEPT POLIT STUDIES/
PETERBOROUGH K9J 7B8/ONTARIO/CANADA/
JOURNAL OF CANADIAN STUDIES, V18, N1,
P136-142, 1983

? ss peterborough/ti and ontario/ti
        2      27 PETERBOROUGH/TI
        3     789 ONTARIO/TI
        4       1 2 AND 3
? t 4/5/1
729624  ARTICLE OATS ORDER#:  DD920  11
  REFS SEASONAL - VARIATIONS IN IMPACT OF
  SUBURBAN DEVELOPMENT ON RUNOFF RESPONSE -
PETERBOROUGH, ONTARIO (EN)
  TAYLOR CH
  TRENT UNIV,DEPT/GEOG/PETERBOROUGH K9J 7B8
ONTARIO/CANADA/WATER RESOURCES RESEARCH,
V13 N2, P464-468,1977

  BRATER EF (2001C US GEOL SURV W, 1969)
  DUNNE T (HYDROL SCI B, V20,P305,1975)
  HARRIS EE (1951B US GEOL SURV W, 1964)
  HOLLIS GE (WAT RESOUR RES, V11, P431,
              1975)
  LEOPOLD LB (554 US GEOL SURV CIR, 1968)
  MOORE WL (EFFECTS WATERSHED CH, V1, 1969)
  SAWYER RM (475C US GEOL SURV PR, P185,
              1963)
  SEABURN GE (627B US GEOL SURV PR, 1969)
  WAANANEN AO (424C US GEOL SURV PR, PC353,
              1961)
  WIITALA SW (ASPECTS EFFECT URBAN, 1961)
  WILSON KV (575D US GEOL SURV PR, PD259,
              1967)
```

Fig. 12. Example from Social Scisearch

```
                68-84/JUN
             Set Items Description
             --- ----- -----------

        ? s peterborough and ontario
                 64 PETERBOROUGH
               3714 ONTARIO
            3    11 PETERBOROUGH AND ONTARIO
        ? t 3/3/1-11

        3/3/6

        0848829 LCCN:  80509271 //r84
           Natl. Bibliography No.: C***
           The Holy Land, a history of Ennismore
        Township, county of Peterborough, Ontario,
        1825-1975 / Clare F. Galvin (The History
        of Ennismore Research Committee)
           Galvin, Clare F.
           Corporate Source:  History of Ennismore
        Research Committee.
           [Ennismore, Ont.] : Township of
        Ennismore c1978.  viii, 334 p.: ill. ;
        24cm.
           Publication Date(s): 1978
           LC Call No.: F1059.5.E55G34  Dewey Call
        No.: 971.3/67
```

Fig. 13.   Example from LC MARC.File426:LC MARC - 68-84/JUN

The expand command is necessary in this case since the form of the cited reference in the data base may vary. Expand tells us what the various forms are. In this case none of the authors from the search of Dissertation Abstracts Online proved useful. Luckily, I found a reference in a book to a master's thesis by G.R. Ferguson (1979) which Brunger cited and Social Scisearch pick up. Brunger's article which was published in 1982 (citation indexes allowed me to move forward in time) possibly would have been overlooked had it not cited Ferguson. As it turned out, it was very relevant focusing on the county of Peterborough.

INFORMATION ON GENEALOGY AND LOCAL HISTORY

A search of DIALINDEX plugging in the words geneal? or (history and local) uncovered some rather surprising sources of genealogical information. Using the information science file group, we found the information shown in figure 17.

```
File38:  America: History & Life - 63-84/
Iss21C (Copr. ABC Clio Inc.)
     Set Items Description
     --- ----- -----------
? ss peterboro or peterborough
          1     0 PETERBORO
          2    15 PETERBOROUGH
          3    15 1 OR 2
? ss s3 and ontario
          4  1741 ONTARIO
          5     9 3 AND 4
? t 5/3/1-9
5/3/3
   545776     14B-02335
   Illustrated Historical Atlas of
Peterborough County, 1825-1875.
   Osborne, Brian ; Atlas, Historical
Peterborough Historical Atlas Foundation
Board.
   Source: Peterborough, Ont.:  Peterborough
Hist. Atlas Foundation, 1975.  127 pp.
? ss (irish or ireland) and immigration?
          6   931 IRISH
          7   395 IRELAND
          8  2298 IMMIGRATION?
          9   104 (4 or 5) AND 6

? ss s9 and (ontario or canada)
         10  1741 ONTARIO
         11  8943 CANADA
         12    14 9 AND (10 OR 11)

? t 12/3/1-14

12/3/5
    577869     20A-03762
    GEOGRAPHICAL PORPINQUITY AMONG PRE-FAMINE
CATHOLIC IRISH SETTLERS IN UPPER CANADA.
    Brunger, Alan G.
    J. of Hist. Geog. 1982 8(3): 265-282.
12/3/8
    536974  18A-00325
    IRISH IMMIGRATION TO CANADA IN THE
NINETEENTH CENTURY.
    Stortz, Gerald J. Stortz, Gerald J.
    Immigration Hist. Newsletter 1979 11
(2):  9-13
```

Fig. 14.   Example from America: History and Life

```
                Set Items Description
                --- ----- -----------
? ss (irish or ireland) and (canada or
  ontario)
            4    606 IRISH
            5    389 IRELAND
            6   2315 CANADA
            7   1065 ONTARIO
            8     15 (4 OR 5) AND (6 OR 7)

? ss s8 and immigration
            9    472 IMMIGRATION
           10      0 8 AND 9
? t 8/3/1-15
8/3/1
849918 ORDER NO:  NOT AVAILABLE FROM
UNIVERSITY MICROFILMS INT'L UNSKILLED
LABOURERS ON THE PUBLIC WORKS OF CANADA,
1840-1880 BLEASDALE, RUTH ELISABETH (PH.D.
1984 THE UNIVERSITY OF WESTERN ONTARIO
(CANADA).
PAGE 1493 IN VOLUME 45/05-A OF DISSERTATION
ABSTRACTS INTERNATIONAL.

8/3/14 543372  ORDER NO: AAD75-29124
   The IRISH IN CANADA, 1815-1867.  399 PAGES
   NOLTE, WILLIAM MICHAEL (PH.D 1975
UNIVERSITY OF MARYLAND).  PAGE 3935 IN
VOLUME 36/06-A OF DISSERTATION ABSTRACTS
INTERNATIONAL.
```

Fig. 15.   Example from Dissertation Abstracts Online

ERIC particularly turned out to be a rich source of articles about genealogy. A sample is shown in figure 18.

As previously stated, most existing data bases are not designed for historical use, but even so, some of them may still have some genealogical value, and particularly if any ancestors being searched were prominent in a field covered by one of these data bases or, for example, invented something. This means that many of these existing data bases can thus be used indirectly. We will name a couple more obvious of these uses.

One use, for example, would be to rapidly find people of the same surname worldwide. This is possible because so many of these data bases are international in scope.

Another use would be to find the biographies which, again, are more international in scope. Chemical

```
              File7:SOCIAL SCISEARCH - 72-85/WK02
              (Copr. ISI Inc.)
                   Set Items Description
                   --- ----- -----------
   ? e cr=ferguson gr
   Ref Items  Index-term
   E1      1  CR=FERGUSON GO, 1916
   E2      1  CR=FERGUSON GO, 1920,
                 V3, P47
   E3         *CR=FERGUSON GR
   E4      1  CR=FERGUSON GR, 1979
   E5      1  CR=FERGUSON GS, 1934
   E6      1  CR=FERGUSON GS, 1976
   E7      3  CR=FERGUSON GT, 1971,
                 V45, P62
   E8      1  CR=FERGUSON GV, 1935,
                 V15, P247
   ? s e4
                  1      1 CR=FERGUSON GR, 1979
   ? t 1/3/1
   1/3/1 1503300   OATS ORDER#: NX181  41 REFS
     GEOGRAPHICAL PORPINQUITY AMONG PRE-FAMINE
   CATHOLIC IRISH SETTLERS IN UPPER CANADA (EN)
     BRUNGERS AG
     TRENT UNIV, DEPT GEOG/PETERBOROUGH K9J
     7B8/ONTARIO/CANADA/JOURNAL OF HISTORICAL
     GEOGRAPHY, V8, N3, P265-282, 1982
```

Fig. 16. Example from Social Scisearch

Abstracts, a chemical data base, for example, contains quite a bit of biographical material on chemists, and certainly would be a helpful source for somebody whose family has had chemist connections in the past.

THE FUTURE OF ONLINE GENEALOGICAL SEARCHING

Besides these existing data bases, it is certain that more and more data based associated with the humanities will appear which will directly benefit historians and genealogists. As the price of putting up a data base goes down, we should see more historical societies and other non-profit organizations putting up their own data bases benefiting genealogists. Right now, the National Genealogical Society is investigating the possibilities of putting up a data base.

In fact, if members of local historical and

```
? s files infosci
File1:ERIC - 66-84/Dec
File6:NTIS - 64-85/Iss03
File12:INSPEC - 1969 thru 1976
File13:INSPEC - 77-85/Iss02
File61:LISA - 69-84(8410)
File202:INFORMATION SCIENCE ABSTRACTS
66-84/Aug
        File Items Description
        ---- ----- -----------
? s geneal? or history and local
        (1) [ERIC--1966 to last update]
                97 GENEAL?
             30158 HISTORY
             20494 LOCAL
              1861 GENEAL? OR (HISTORY AND
                      LOCAL)
        (6) [NTIS--1964 to last update]
                36 GENEAL?
             23043 HISTORY
             37411 LOCAL
              1785 GENEAL? OR (HISTORY AND
                      LOCAL)
            [INSPEC--1969 to 1976]
                29 GENEAL?
              4975 HISTORY
             18234 LOCAL
               127 GENEAL? OR (HISTORY AND
                      LOCAL)
        (13) [INSPEC--1977 to last update]
                57 GENEAL?
              9425 HISTORY
             35214 LOCAL
               280 GENEAL? OR (HISTORY AND
                      LOCAL)
        (61) [LISA--1969 to last update]
                52 GENEAL?
              3446 HISTORY
              3198 LOCAL
               381 GENEAL? OR (HISTORY AND
                      LOCAL)
        (202) [INFORMATION SCIENCE ABSTRACTS]
                80 GENEAL?
              2302 HISTORY
              2309 LOCAL
               179 GENEAL? OR (HISTORY AND
                      LOCAL)
```

Fig. 17.   Example from DIALINDEX

```
File1:ERIC - 66-84/Dec
     Set Items Description
     ---  -----  -----------

? ss geneal? or (local(w)history)
      1    97 GENEAL?
      2   567 LOCAL(w)HISTORY
      3   635 1 OR (2)

? t 1/3/1-10
1/3/1 EJ304531
  Genealogy and Libraries.
  Carothers, Diane Foxhill; And Others
  Library Trends, v32 n1 p1-159 Sum 1983

1/3/5  EJ295530
  Improved Genealogical Reference Services
through Automation:  The LDS Genealogical
Library.
  Clement, Charles
  RQ, v23 n2 p202-09 Win
  1983
  Available from:  UMI

1/3/6 EJ295529
  Searching for Genealogies in the Library
of Congress Computer Catalog.
  Reid, Judith P.
  RQ, v23 n2 p195-201 Win
  1983
  Available from: UMI

1/3/7  EJ295528
  Passenger and Naturalization Lists:  The
New Sources.
  Filby, P. William
  RQ, v 23 n2 p189-94 Win
  1983
  Available from: UMI
```

Fig. 18.   Example from ERIC

genealogical societies were to use computers or word
processors in making up their articles of genealogical
value, duplicate machine-readable copies could easily be
sent to some larger society for incorporation into a data
base. Similarly, even small organizations could put up
computer bulletin boards which could be accessed by
genealogists all over the country.

Another thing we may see is that instead of just
containing references to books and articles, we'll see
data bases in which the entire journal or book text is
available online. This is already occurring in certain
fields such as chemistry. Today the dozen journals put
out by the American Chemical Society are available online
in their entirety. Likewise, the popular journals and
newspapers such as Newsweek and Time, New York Times,
Washington Post, UPI dispatches, etc.

OCLC, Inc. is presently working on a project to
collect the machine-readable manuscripts from publishers
after they print their books and use the table of contents
and indexes to produce a more precise subject approach to
the retrieval of information in books. In addition, if
problems of copyright can be worked out, full text online
retrieval might be offered.

As the cost goes down, and the technology for
information storage continues to improve, inevitably more
and more information in its entirety will likewise become
available online. Right now I have a cartoon in my office
picturing a man asking the librarian if he can have the
library's chemistry collection on a laser disk to check
out. This may appear funny to use now, but possibilities
such as this become less and less remote as time goes on.

Now, in considering future possibilities, what if the
Genealogical Society of Salt Lake (and I use them because
they are one of the few nonprofit organizations putting
lots of money into this kind of thing) decided to store
their original records on disks, rather than on
microfilm? And say the New York Public Library, or the
Library of Congress (which is considering this), or other
libraries with the aid of optical readers, decided to
store the contents of their old, valuable, but rapidly
deteriorating books on laser disks, or some other machine
readable form. Suddenly, you have the situation where not
just the reference to your desired book is available, but
the entire text. Only now the value of each of these
texts is increased many times because of the greatly
increased number of access points, as we have previously
discussed. Yes, every single name, number, date, map,
picture, portrait, and lineage chart found in any of these
online books becomes instantly available.

What are the implications for your research? Of course, they are enormous. Let us imagine you entering such a modernized library. You'll be able to instantly find what you're looking for, not just the reference to it, but the whole material itself. Instead of somebody saying, "I'm sorry, but that book is not on the shelf," you'll get that information on a computer terminal, with the option of printing hardcopy on the spot to take home for your research files.

In fact, with equipment that will then exist in your own home, you won't need to go the the public library. Instead you'll be able to call up. That book housed on a disk in the New York Public Library will be instantaneously transmitted over fiber optical lines into your own home where you can read, sort out, and copy just what you need, saving not only time but all the money and hassles of traveling to New York City.

The challenge of the future, then, may not be not finding enough information on your research project, but rather finding too much information, thus calling for a whole new set of research techniques. We already have this same situation in the field of chemistry, in which most of my experience lies. Here the challenge is finding the information you need, hidden amongst similar information you don't need. You don't want every article or book dealing with plastics, just as you don't want information on every John Smith born in the city of New York. And so these searches for information must be thoughtfully designed so that unwanted information is trimmed away, and yet not so much that something of value is lost.

I am certain that just as data bases have increased each year in the sciences and business world, data bases will appear in the world of genealogy and local history. These new data bases will offer great opportunities as well as new challenges to genealogists.

BIBLIOGRAPHY

Falk, Joyce Duncan. "America: History and Life Online: History and Much More," Database, 6 (2): 1983 14-25.

Kilgour, Frederick G.; Kiser, Betsy; and Brown, Georgia. "An Electronic Information Delivery Online System." In 8th International Online Information Meeting, London, 4-6 Dec 1984, pp. 331-342. Oxford, N.J. : Learned Information, 1985.

Sweetland, James H. "America : History and Life -- A Wide Ranging Database." Database, 6(4) (1983) : 15-29.